SOLDIER OF THE ANDES
José de San Martín
(1778-1850)

Many of the striking paradoxes of South America are embodied in the story of one of her greatest heroes. José de San Martín was a soldier who fought against the Spanish army that trained him, a general who led a war for liberty but did not fully trust democracy and a patriot who died in self-imposed exile, scorned by the very countries he helped create. San Martín is rivaled only by Simon Bolívar as an architect of South American independence.

BOOKS BY PAUL RINK

IN DEFENSE OF FREEDOM
The Story of the Monroe Doctrine

THE LAND DIVIDED, THE WORLD UNITED
The Story of the Panama Canal

QUEST FOR FREEDOM
Bolívar and the South American Revolution

SOLDIER OF THE ANDES
José de San Martín

SOLDIER
of the
ANDES

José de San Martín

by Paul Rink

JULIAN MESSNER
NEW YORK

Published by Julian Messner, a division of Simon & Schuster, Inc., 1 West 39 Street, New York, N.Y. 10018. All rights reserved.

Ju V
F
2235.4
R63

Printed in the United States of America
ISBN 0–671–32383–0 Cloth Trade
        0–671–32384–9 MCE
Library of Congress Catalog Card No. 76–140677

Ca

SOLDIER OF THE ANDES

José de San Martín

Chapter 1

JULY 9, 1789. The post coach from Málaga neared the end of its long journey up from the coast to the high central plateau of Spain. The excited passengers held aside the leather curtains, their eager eyes peering ahead, anxious for a glimpse of the city which was slowly coming into view. At last it lay before them—Madrid, the magic city, capital of the greatest empire in the world—its towers, castles and spires gleaming beneath the blue Spanish sky.

The coach rumbled through the gates, the shoes of its weary horses clattering on the cobbles. The iron rims of the heavy wheels ground over the stones, sending echoes flying down narrow alleys, across fountained and flowered plazas, from the balconies of private residences.

On the coach went, deeper into the city, the noise of its passage and the cries of its driver scattering pedestrians like pigeons. At last it slowed and stopped in front of an enormous long two-story barracks. The grim stone walls of the building came flush with the street and were bare, without windows or openings of any kind except for a huge oaken doorway wide enough for a troop of cavalry to come through at full gallop if necessary. This door was now open and gave a glimpse of a big indoor patio and parade ground.

The driver of the coach tumbled a leather trunk from the roof of the vehicle to the ground. One of the passengers, a small boy, descended, and the coach clattered off. The boy was left alone, fidgeting under the suspicious glare of a sentry lounging at the guard post. He presented a paper and in a moment was inside the building, walking along broad corridors and at last up a very wide and shallow stairway to the second floor. Ahead of him stalked a guide, and behind came another soldier, the boy's leather trunk swinging easily on his shoulders.

They entered an enormous room, with rough oaken floors and walls of stone on which were hung guidon pennants and battle flags. The room was empty except for a large table at one end. Behind the table sat the colonel who commanded the regiment. His adjutant stood beside him. The table was littered with papers.

The colonel was a huge man, with a browned and seamed face scarred with saber cuts. His fierce dark eyes stared sourly at the boy standing before the table. The boy looked strong; he was deep-chested with broad shoulders, and carried himself well, but there was something about him that the colonel did not like. The eyes were too dark—nearly black—and so was the hair, and the skin of his face was too deep a brown. "Almost like a cursed Indian," the colonel muttered under his breath.

The boy heard the remark. He stiffened, and a flush of embarrassment stained his cheeks, but he said nothing.

"Thy name?" grunted the colonel.

"José de San Martín, at your orders, *Señor Coronel*." The voice was clear and polite, and grave. "Born February 25, 1778."

"Thine age?" There was no friendliness in the colonel's tones.

"Eleven years, *Señor*."

The colonel shook his head slightly, almost in disgust. Then he pawed with huge, ungainly fingers through the papers on the table, found the one he was looking for and scanned it briefly, all the while throwing angry glances at the boy.

The form which he read was addressed to the Marquis de Zaya, and had been approved by the Count de Bornos. Among other things it said, "Following the example of my father and my cadet brothers, who are serving in the Soria Regiment, I wish to pursue the distinguished career of the army and my father is ready to provide for my upkeep according to His Majesty's regulations."

The colonel threw one last glance at the boy and then dismissed him with a curt flick of the hand. The boy walked swiftly out of the room, following the soldier who was carrying his trunk.

The colonel looked up at his adjutant. "I don't like it," he said disdainfully.

The adjutant shrugged. He picked up the papers on the table and read from those parts covering the sections on the investigation done by the Inquisition on the boy's ancestry: ". . . and he is free from evil strains of the Moor, the heretic or of any Jew recently converted to our Holy Catholic Church; and neither has his family ever been in trouble with the Holy Office of the Inquisition."

"The record is clean, sir," said the adjutant. "His father has had a very honorable although completely undistinguished career in the army as an Indian fighter and military administrator in the Americas, and is currently port captain at Málaga. His brothers as well as the male ancestors on his mother's side have excellent service records also."

"Don't doubt it. Don't doubt it in any way," grunted the colonel. "There is nothing wrong with these *hidalgo* families. The army has need of them. But this one . . ." His voice trailed off in disgust. "This one—*born* in the Americas. It is too much." Then the man quoted an ancient saying, "Were there but one mule driver left in La Mancha, he would be more fit to govern the Americas than the greatest noble born in the colonies."

He was silent a moment; the adjutant waited respectfully. Then he continued. "Americans—I do not trust them. Inevitably the moment comes when their loyalties revert to the land of their birth. Yes. No matter this boy's ancestry. No matter his blood lines, pure though they may be. The important thing is that he was born in La Plata. He is South American–Argentinian. He is not Spanish no matter what the records say." He looked up at the adjutant and repeated, "He is American, not Spanish."

The purity of ancestry and the loyalty of officers in his beloved Murcia Regiment must never be open to the slightest suspicion. The regiment was one of Spain's oldest and most honorable, and now it was reduced to taking officer cadets who had been born in the Americas.

The old soldier sighed, his thoughts taking secret pathways which could have cost him his head had he uttered them aloud. Without any question whatsoever, the colonel would have laid down his life for the Spanish throne and his church, but he was also aware of the decay in Spanish society. Daily it confronted him—the indecisiveness, the weakness, the near-imbecility of those who governed the nation. Spain's iron-willed kings and queens, the soldiers, statesmen and churchmen who had made the nation great in the past, were gone. In their places were people who were corrupt, whose spendthrift regime milked the country dry, whose self-centered, wavering policies made her the derision of the rest of Europe, the victim of the whimsies of stronger nations. There was not even enough money or strength of purpose to train army officers properly. All the academies but one had been closed, and even had they existed, the dissolute aristocracy no longer produced tough-fibered boys out of which fighting army officers could be made. The colonel sniffed in frustration and disgust. Heaven knew these young colonial boys were of a different stripe—but what matter, if they could not be trusted? How could anyone who had not first seen the light in Spain be considered a true Spaniard?

The colonel broke off his dangerous reverie. He looked up at his adjutant. "Well, sir," he said, "there's nothing to be done. This is what we've got—Americans, colonials. See if you can make a Spanish soldier out of him."

Thus it was that at the age of eleven, José de San Martín, an American born in far-off La Plata, donned the white and azure uniform of an officer cadet in the Spanish Peninsular Army. His family had come home to Spain

when he was five years old and had managed to find
enough money for a few years' schooling in a "nobles'
seminary." This was the end of his education. From now
on the rough world of the barracks, the garrison and the
bivouacs of numberless campaigns became his home. The
life of a soldier became his life and the savage school of
the battlefield his only classroom. Spain lost no time in
providing the boy with the opportunity to learn the profession of arms; there was little about soldiering that her
wars could not teach him.

José de San Martín first saw service in Africa, at
Melilla, just across the Mediterranean from Spain. There
rebellious and fierce desert tribesmen kept the Murcia
Regiment under almost continual attack; but this was
nothing compared to what was coming.

The ancient city of Oran, some miles along the coast
from Melilla, has had as bloody a history as any city in
the world. It was first settled by adventurous Spanish
sailors from Andalusia in the tenth century. Since that
time Spaniards, Arabs, Turks and Moors had waged con-
tinuous warfare for its possession. In 1732 it was taken
by the Turks, but the terrible cruelties inflicted by them
on the large Spanish population forced Spain to recapture
the city. Spanish troops held it until 1791, when it again
came under furious attacks by Moors.

When the attack began, the Murcia Regiment was sent
immediately from Melilla to Oran. Young San Martín
was ordered to join a company of grenadiers fighting with
his regiment. The battle lasted for two days without stop
in blinding heat. The men endured constant artillery
shelling and repulsed wave after wave of attacking in-

fantry and cavalry. The horror of the battle was increased by a terrible earthquake during the height of the struggle. When the attackers finally withdrew in defeat, there was nothing left of Oran except broken walls and dead and wounded people.

This experience was a stern initiation for José de San Martín to the brutal savagery of war. It scarred him deeply. For the rest of his life he was aware of the sad necessity for war at times, but he was forever cured of any belief in the glory of martial exploits, or in the nobility of battle. He was scarcely thirteen years old when his romantic dreams and ideals of combat perished in the heat and rubble of Oran.

While young José de San Martín was enduring his initial baptism to war in Africa, back in Europe forces far greater than anything the world had ever known before were building. Soon they exploded into a storm that released a hurricane of fury and battle. The earth of Europe trembled to the tramp of millions upon millions of marching men, and its skies echoed to the thunder of the struggle. The land ran red with rivers of blood, and the butchery spread without reason or cause to places as far distant as Egypt and Russia. There would be no peace until the world was spent and exhausted and could fight no more. The carnage was to last until June of 1815, when Napoleon was defeated at Waterloo.

These were the years, beginning in 1789, of the birth of the French Republic, and of the stirrings of men everywhere for enlightenment and freedom from ancient oppressions. These were the years when a new idea ap-

peared, the idea that men could learn to govern themselves and did not have to submit to the tyranny of kings
and queens, or that of the rich, landed aristocracy. The
old regimes, basing their rights on the theory that they
were God-given, fought back with all their strength.

These were years of high purpose, and of betrayal, of
astounding heroism and the vilest cowardice. In some
lands democracy triumphed. In others the old systems
emerged from the holocaust with even greater power.
And in still others, as in Spain, tottering and treacherous
monarchies fell and others still more vicious rose in
their places, currying favor with whichever side seemed
stronger and abandoning to the wolves the helpless
peoples they ruled. The emergence of freedom and
democracy did not come easily in Europe. Its birth was
filled with pain.

In Africa, young José de San Martín was at first in profound ignorance of such matters. He was too busy trying
to learn the rudiments of his profession, obeying orders
and, above all, keeping himself alive to be concerned
about such events. Soon, however, this was changed
drastically. Spain was hopelessly caught up in a military
hurricane; the Murcia Regiment was ordered home, and
for twenty years San Martín was in the center of a
holocaust.

In the shifting balance of alliances caused by Spain's
decadence and wavering foreign policy, the enemies of
today were more than apt to be the allies of tomorrow.
Thus it was that Spanish troops fought French Repub-
lican armies across the Pyrenees Mountains in France.
They fought the British at sea while stationed aboard the

ships of Spain's Mediterranean squadron. They first battled against the Portuguese and then later fought beside them as comrades in arms. Then they were allied with the British when England sent soldiers to Spain to fight Napoleon and his dreams of imperial conquest.

Finally, at the climax of the Peninsular Wars, Spanish and British armies together went down in defeat before the legions of Napoleon, who became master of all of Spain, with no one to oppose him but the Spanish people and their shattered armies. Alone they faced the grizzled and seasoned French veterans.

Spain may have been defeated on the battlefield, but her people were not demoralized. When Napoleon put his brother Joseph as puppet king on the Spanish throne, the reaction was instant and violent. The government and the royal family were rotten and had fallen apart like a house of cards, but the tough-fibered Spanish people were something entirely different. Their King Ferdinand had been an ineffectual and traitorous monarch, but he was theirs. Bad as he was, they were in no mood to exchange him for an upstart Frenchman.

Committees were set up to rule the country and to administer the colonies. In remote places of the country they functioned as best they could. The broken armies managed to pull themselves together, and to a man the people rose up to resist the French. The soldiers were untrained, half-clothed; they had no money for weapons or for ammunition, and yet they found the courage and the strength to fight against this desecration of their land. They could not defeat the French decisively—no power on earth at this time could have successfully challenged Napoleon. Yet so well did they storm his fortresses and battle his troops in chaotic, large-scale guerrilla enounters that in later years Napoleon wrote, "Spain was a running sore that sapped my strength."

Nevertheless, Napoleon's star was rising over Europe. As it rose, Spain's problems and her humiliation deepened. As the nations of Europe armed and formed alliances to strike at France, more and more what was left of Spain became a helpless pawn caught in a struggle of giants. In spite of the heroic efforts of her people, the Spanish armies were decimated and increasingly had to operate as semi-official guerrilla bands. The last remnants of her once powerful fleet were sunk by Nelson at Trafalgar. To strike at England, Napoleon forced Spain to cede to him the enormous territory of Louisiana in North America, which he then promptly sold for a pittance to the infant United States. Finally, insisting that Spain was "no more," Napoleon claimed that her colonies in the Americas belonged to him, and sent representatives to the New World to back up his claim. The Americans sent these emissaries packing. Inevitably, however, these colonials began asking themselves a crucial question: If Spain, their motherland, no longer existed, then to whom did the colonies now really belong?

As Spain's fortunes declined and her troubles deepened at home, so also the problems in the colonies began to multiply. The reaction at first was the same as in Spain. Committees, or *juntas,* were organized for the purpose of administering and preserving the empire until such time as King Ferdinand could resume his rightful place on the throne. People renewed their oaths of loyalty. They raised money to buy arms to defend themselves. They rushed about emotionally, wearing armbands which proclaimed their willingness to "die for good King Ferdinand" should it be necessary

Nevertheless, the people in Spain's vast colonies were beginning to awaken and to seethe with unrest. The winds of freedom and of liberty which blew in Europe wafted across the Atlantic, and they whispered seductively. Old grievances and resentments in the Americas clamored for solutions which demanded far more wisdom than anything which Spain's faltering leadership could provide.

The colonies of Spanish America were divided into four gigantic areas called viceroyalties, literally "vice-kingdoms." That to the north was called New Spain, and included the enormous territories which are now a part of the United States, Mexico and the Central American Republics as far as the Isthmus of Panama. Below this lay New Granada, made up of what are now Venezuela, Colombia and sections of Ecuador. Next came the viceroyalty of Peru, bounded by the Pacific on one side and the towering peaks of the Andes mountains on the other. Out of this area eventually emerged the modern nations of Chile and Peru and certain parts of Bolivia. And farther south and to the east was the stupendous land mass of La Plata, composed of modern Argentina, Paraguay, Uruguay and sections of Bolivia.

The peoples throughout this fantastic chunk of our globe's surface were divided roughly into four large strata. At the top of the heap were the *Peninsulares,* men from the Iberian Peninsula—that is, Spanish-born Spaniards. Next were the Creoles, children of the Spanish who had been born in the colonies. Below these were the *Mestizos*, people of mixed blood. At the very bottom of the pile were the indigenous people, the Indians.

These four layers divided the population of the colonies into a very rigid caste system. Each layer was in general at odds with the others, if not bitter enemies, and most were kept in a state of deep ignorance by Spain. The most numerous groups—the *Mestizos* and the Indians—were the worst off of all, poverty-stricken and relegated to positions which in many cases were close to slavery.

For centuries Spain had sealed off her empire from the rest of the world. Her edicts of isolation were backed up by the world's most powerful military forces. The system had worked well, but by 1810 the sparks of discontent had ignited; the tinder was ready to burst into full flame. Many young Creoles had been sent to Europe for an education, and when they returned home they were appalled at the ignorance and the backwardness of their homelands and brought with them word of social change and of enlightenment. It fell on ears which were ready to listen.

At this precise moment in history, the events in Europe offered a God-given opportunity to those who had been infected with the "virus" of freedom for the colonies. And it was precisely the young people—the disaffected young Creoles who, because of the accident of their having been born in the colonies, were denied any part in their own destinies—who sparked the fires of revolt. In spite of many confusing and false starts, the wars of rebellion in Spanish America turned into a struggle between

young, hotheaded, patriotic Creoles, aided by *Mestizos,*
and *Peninsulares,* aided by wealthy, conservative and
older Creoles.

During all these years of bitter fighting and chaos in
Spain, and of mounting restlessness in the colonies, José
de San Martín served his country loyally and well. Without question he fought Spain's enemies wherever and
whenever he was ordered. On endless battlefields he was
on intimate terms with deprivation, despair, cold and
hunger. He tasted victory, and he knew bitter defeat as
well. From the continual campaigning, with nights which
he spent sleeping on wet, cold ground, he contracted
serious diseases—arthritis and rheumatism. And from the
worry and eternal frustration and battle fatigue, and the
always poor, half-spoiled food which he ate, he developed
acute stomach ulcers. All of these maladies caused him
untold misery for years.

During these twenty long years of combat, San Martín
was wounded and decorated many times. Promotion came
rapidly; he was made a sublieutenant on the battlefield.
When he was seventeen years old, he was again promoted,
this time to full lieutenant. In 1808, by the time he was
thirty, he had risen to the rank of captain, and a short
time later he became a lieutenant-colonel, and was given a
regiment of his own to command. The young cadet who
was an American, and hence "not to be trusted," was
indeed doing very well. In spite of the "unfortunate"
accident of colonial birth, San Martín's life had made
him more European than American. He was Spanish
through and through; he had served his country with

supreme courage and devotion and had been well rewarded by it.

Nevertheless, the faltering, frightened leadership of
that country, with its dissolute rulers, who veered to the
wind with each passing threat and who sold out their
people to the enemy, were not lost on him. Gradually,
the heretical thought began to grow: the figure of the
king was not the divinely inspired and incorruptible
source of law, justice and good which he had been taught
to believe, but was rather a man like all men, and worse
than most in many respects—selfish and evil and in no
sense fit to govern a loyal people.

Most disturbing of all to San Martín was the news
which came across the Atlantic from the Americas. As the
unrest mounted and the fires of rebellion burned brighter
and brighter, his own sense of injustice and outrage increased. Finally he saw clearly that the whole structure of
majesty and aristocracy was a fraud and a sham which had
bled the colonies white for nearly 350 years.

Such shifts in his thinking did not come painlessly to
San Martín. The foundation of his life was built on personal honor and loyalty. Once his word was given, he did
not go back on it. Above all, he was a high officer in the
Spanish Army, and his oath of allegiance to it was bind-
ing. Whatever he was and whatever he had, he owed to
the monarchy of Spain and to the army. It had been his
only home, his only teacher, since the age of eleven.

To question all this was not a simple matter, but nevertheless to his austere and clear mind the questions rose
by themselves, unbidden, to plague him. Eventually he
began to see and to feel, emotionally as well as intellectu-

forces but had been trounced each time. He landed again in 1812 and was once again defeated, captured and taken back to Spain, where he died chained to the wall of a dungeon in Cádiz. The struggle was continued by another Venezuelan Creole, the great Simón Bolívar. He waged war for years against the Spaniards, back and forth from ocean to ocean across the top of the continent.

In Peru no revolt ever flared. Peru remained the richest, most loyal of all the colonies, but in the southern part of the viceroyalty, in Chile, the flames of freedom burned clear and bright, led by such men as the famous patriot Creole, Bernardo O'Higgins. These revolts in Chile were ruthlessly stamped out by Spanish troops sent down from Lima, the capital of the territory.

In La Plata, or Argentina, San Martín's homeland, the situation was vastly more complicated.

For all its boundless potential wealth, the enormous viceroyalty of La Plata had been shabbily treated by the motherland. The area was a neglected stepchild, not even organized into a viceroyalty until long after the others were productive and flourishing. In the normal matters of exploration, military protection and trade, La Plata lagged far behind the rest of the empire.

The principal reason for this was that in La Plata there was very little immediate wealth available. In the early days of exploration and discovery, Spain had had great dreams of finding gold and silver in this part of the empire. *La plata* itself means "silver," and the word Argentina means "silvered." Alas, this dream was an illusion. There was no precious metal to be picked up as in

Mexico or Peru; and because of this so-called metallic poverty, the viceroyalty was not considered worth a great deal of attention.

The Indians there had never advanced to the point where they built flourishing societies and cities, as the native peoples had done in other parts of the empire. They were nomads, ranging wide and free over the vast seas of the pampas, and they were fierce and stubborn warriors who defended themselves with desperate ferocity. Early Spanish attempts to explore the great rivers and prairies of La Plata and establish cities met with tragic disaster.

Mexico City was found by Cortes about 1521 after the destruction of the ancient Aztec city. Lima, in Peru, was laid out by Pizarro in 1532 after he had subdued the Incas. Almost from their beginnings, both these cities were noted for their riches and for their brilliant and luxurious way of life. Buenos Aires, on the other hand, was established in 1536, then abandoned, then re-established in 1580. It did not assume any importance whatsoever until it was made the capital of the viceroyalty in 1776, and even then it continued to be a poverty-stricken and squalid village.

Although there was a lack of gold and silver in La Plata, there was no lack of incredibly rich farmland. In some places the rich black loam is more than eleven feet deep. The endless pampas were early broken up into ranches so enormous that in other parts of the world built on a less grand scale they would have been considered kingdoms. But the only products of these ranches were meat and hides, difficult to transport and of small value when compared with the gold, silver and jewels of Mexico and Peru.

Lonely military garrisons and church missions so remote they were half forgotten in the great, empty land kept the countryside under an easy and lax Spanish control. In all primitive territories, military, political and cultural power tends to concentrate in the cities; and in La Plata this pattern was especially pronounced. In the interior there were only two cities worthy of any note—Córdoba and Mendoza—and they were little more than frontier trading posts. Buenos Aires was located on the coast, near the mouth of the La Plata River. Primitive as the capital was, banishment to the interior towns was considered punishment enough for nearly any crime.

The result of this polarization into the "capital" and the "interior" was that the people of both areas tended to draw away from each other. The inhabitants of the interior expected and got little help in anything from the capital. They learned to depend upon themselves and to look only to themselves when they needed assistance of any kind. Eventually they came to feel that the ties which bound them to Spain were loose and of little consequence. Their lives became relatively free of Spanish control. In Buenos Aires the opposite took place. Here the people looked eastward, to the mother country, accepting without protest official authority and restraint. Thus it was that in La Plata, more than in any other part of the empire, the division between "capital" and "interior" was profound.

This independent state of mind was true of most of the great landowners of the interior, but it was doubly true of the *gauchos*. The *gauchos* were largely landless nomads and *vaqueros* who lived a wild and free life on the pampas. They recognized no man as their master; they existed according to their own codes and had their own ways of managing their affairs. It is not strange that the earliest movements for independence from Spain came from the *gauchos*. One of them, José Artigas, was a legendary bull of a man, free and unchained, hard-riding and hard-drinking. He roamed the pampas which stretched for endless miles across the river from Buenos Aires, and from these vast empty lands, he declared complete independence from Spain. He patterned the nation which he wanted to establish "with the United States of North America as my model." The people on the pampas became so accustomed to running their own affairs, and so estranged from the control of Buenos Aires, that even after freedom was won from Spain and all of Argentina had become independent, they went their own way and established their own countries.

So it was from the very beginning that there was a sharp cleavage between the *porteños*, the people of the "port," Buenos Aires, and those who lived inland. After the revolts from Spain had started, these differences came boiling to the surface. The *gauchos*, the great Creole landed families and even small *Mestizos* were as anxious as the most liberal *porteño* Creoles for freedom from Spanish domination, but at the same time they were in no way ready to start taking orders from those they considered to be effete city people from Buenos Aires. This feeling continued for years after independence had finally been achieved; more than a century was to pass before the differences between the *porteños* and the people of the interior could be reconciled and the population of Argentina welded into one nation.

The struggle for independence actually started earlier in Argentina than it did anywhere else on the continent, and it took a most unusual direction. It had to do with trade.

As we have noted, Spain's policy for governing her enormous empire was to seal it off from the rest of the world. The colonies were permitted to trade only with Spain, in certain instances with each other and always from special seaports along certain routes. From a myopic point of view this was a good idea. It permitted the wealth of the colonies to flow only to Spain and not to enrich any other country but Spain. This was good for the mother country, but it was a policy bitterly resented in the colonies because it stifled natural development. The edicts having to do with trade were the most often flaunted. In the case of La Plata and Buenos Aires in particular, this Spanish-only policy for commerce was carried to an extreme, as were the efforts made to circumvent it.

The port of Buenos Aires was one of the finest seaports in the world and, because of the network of navigable rivers leading inland, was a natural trading and commercial center for the entire land mass behind it—more than 2,300,000 square miles. Official policy for hundreds of years had been to keep the port tightly closed except to an occasional ship flying the Spanish flag. All commerce had to head westward, inland, on muleback, through Indian-infested country and over some of the most frightful mountain trails in the world. The destination of these pack-trains was Lima, Peru, more than 3,000 miles away. There, the goods were loaded on ships, taken to the Isthmus of Panama, unloaded for transportation on mules across the Isthmus and then finally loaded on other ships for the trip across the Atlantic to Spain! Obviously such a route was an absurdity, and more so because of the fact that the products of La Plata were bulky and heavy—hides, salted meat, forest products and the like. Little wonder that shippers in Buenos Aires and producers in the interior had for centuries clamored for direct shipping service to Spain.

This clamor became so loud that at last, in 1777, frequent and regular shipping service was granted. Immediately Buenos Aires and the pampas ranchers began to prosper. However, as was so often the case in Spain's relations with her colonies, the concessions came too late because over the years the *porteños* had mastered the fine art of smuggling. They continued the practice, trading legally with Spain and illegally with the rest of Europe.

The particular market for Argentina was England. England could supply just about every manufactured item which La Plata needed at cheap prices. Spain's industrial capacity was medieval; she could supply almost nothing at any price. Furthermore, England could absorb, at high prices, all the hides and salted meat which La Plata could produce. It was an example of a perfect trading partnership.

The *porteños* and interior ranchers smelled these sweet profits. They contemplated their warehouses overflowing with goods worth a fortune if they could be gotten into the holds of English ships. They had increased trade with Spain, but it was nowhere enough to satisfy them; they never stopped their clamor for unrestricted trade with the whole world, but in the meantime they kept their lines of communication open with the captains of British contrabanders, which swarmed like mosquitoes along the coasts. Smuggling increased.

By now the confused situation in Europe began to be felt in the Americas. Spain's faltering economy and government became less and less able to supply even a minimum of needs to the traders of Buenos Aires. At the same time, about 1806, Napoleon had most of Europe under his control, and England's trade there was cut to almost nothing. England desperately needed raw materials and just as desperately needed markets for her manufactured goods. La Plata was a natural answer to the dilemma.

William Pitt, one of England's most famous Prime Ministers, was overlooking no opportunities. Before anything else, Pitt understood his country's vital need for unrestricted, world-wide trade. He took one look at Spain's tottering government, another look at La Plata, bulging with everything England needed, and made up his mind what to do.

Nothing so crass or dangerous as an invasion was in his mind. He simply let it be known to the Admiral of the British Atlantic Fleet, Sir Home Popham, that nobody in His Majesty's Government would complain if certain events took place. Popham didn't need any official orders. He knew exactly what to do. He landed in Buenos Aires with 1,700 well-equipped British marines and bluejackets. In no time they had the situation completely under control, taking a half-million pesos in gold which belonged to the Spanish Government. The money was shipped home to London. On the scene, the astonished *porteños* were guaranteed better government, better schools and—the biggest plum—free trade with anyone. It was a very tidy operation.

Then, however, William Pitt died, and in the complicated way of international politics, the new British government washed its hands of the entire affair. Popham was called back to England and his acts disavowed. A year later, another switch took place. England reversed its position and sent an official invasion force to "liberate" La Plata from Spain!

This time the *porteños* were not so flabbergasted at the appearance of the English war fleet. In spite of the tempting bait of free trade and the possibility of being liberated from Madrid without so much as lifting a finger, they were in no mood to exchange Spanish rule for English. Under the leadership of Santiago Liniers, a French soldier-of-fortune, they closed ranks and evicted the British after some sharp fighting. A second English force, more powerful than the first, tried another landing, but was defeated. As the British fleet beat back out to sea from the harbor, one of its ships had the ill luck to run aground on the mud flats. Expert Argentine horsemen galloped out and captured her. This may be the first and time in history when a man-of-war was taken by cavalry.

During all this excitement, the Spanish Viceroy had been of little help. At the first sign of shooting he fled Buenos Aires to safety in the interior. Now he returned, prepared once again to take up his duties. The furious *porteños* loaded him on the first ship bound for Spain and elected Santiago Liniers in his place.

As in other parts of the empire, a *junta* was chosen. At first, as everywhere else, this *junta* tried to act as a trustee to keep the viceroyalty intact for the hapless King Ferdinand. Soon, however, following the pattern, it came to be dominated by Creoles, who advocated independence from Spain.

Although the *junta* struggled desperately, its efforts to unite the country were doomed. The recent emergency with the British had brought all factions of the population together, but once it was over, peace vanished! Creoles, *Peninsulares*, liberals, reactionaries, *Mestizos*, royalists, churchmen, *porteños*, interior people, advocates of free trade, advocates of trade only with Spain and many other groups all vociferously demanded their "rights" to the exclusion of everyone else.

The *junta* did its best to work out compromises which would keep all the various factions content, but it was hopeless. Fighting soon broke out. Everyone was at each other's throats and apparently willing to die for their causes.

As might be imagined, the military forces available to the *junta* were small and weak. Force, wielded by the government, was the only thing which might have kept the peace, but it didn't exist. Slowly at first, and then more quickly, the enormous viceroyalty began to break up, fragmenting first around the outer edges, where effective control of any kind was impossible.

During this period the areas across the La Plata River from Buenos Aires broke away and ultimately became

the Republics of Uruguay and Paraguay. Freedom from
Argentina by no means brought peace to these areas. The
route to independence was a hard one for their people.
They had to beat off loyal monarchistic attacks. They
had to beat off the forces sent by the *junta* in Buenos
Aires to force them back into place. And, in addition,
they had to contend with invasion forces coming down
from Brazil. The Portuguese there knew an opportunity
when they saw one and lost no time in trying to expand
their territory.

So, in spite of their best efforts, the various *juntas* which
came and went in Buenos Aires were unable to stop the
breakup of the viceroyalty. They simply did not have
enough military power to do the job. They were able to
keep the area around Buenos Aires, as well as the pampas
to the west, from splintering off, but much valuable territory was lost forever.

As though the hard-pressed *juntas* didn't have enough
trouble, a new and far more dangerous threat now appeared. The very heart of monarchal power in South
America was in Peru. Here was stationed the flower of
Spanish military might, completely loyal to the homeland. These forces had already totally squashed a rebellion in Chile, and they wasted no time in moving against
the revolutionaries in La Plata. They began to assemble
for a march southward to extinguish what they considered
to be a minor outburst in a distant and primitive corner
of the empire. Once Buenos Aires had been subdued,
their commanders reasoned, they would restore tranquility at their leisure throughout the rest of the entire
traitorous viceroyalty.

During all the years these momentous events were taking place in Spain, across the ocean San Martín's star continued to rise in the Spanish Army. With each promotion his authority and responsibilities in the army increased. But it was not only for valor on the battlefield and for dedication to Spain that his prestige mounted.

José de San Martín was a most unusual type of officer. Most high-ranking officers in those times came from the titled aristocracy. In general they were content to be strutting dandies, fancy figures who postured in gaudy uniforms and danced constant attendance on the ladies. The grim and bloody work of fighting and killing was left to those less nobly born.

San Martín was not this kind of a soldier. He would have none of this sort of hypocrisy for himself. He was a stern, austere disciplinarian who tolerated no nonsense from his men but, at the same time, with each passing year he became more and more a "soldier's soldier." He lived with his troops, fought with them, endured their miseries as his own. But more than this, every aspect of his profession fascinated him, and he studied constantly. He brought to these studies an intelligence and inquisitiveness which kept him up at night, year after year, absorbing everything that was known at the time about the military arts.

Such matters as tactics, logistics and the handling of troops came naturally to him. He was a born leader, with a built-in grasp of such matters, but in his studying he went far beyond basic military skills. He delved into the mathematics of artillery fire, the chemistry of explosives, the metallurgy of iron and brass used for making sabers, muskets and cannon. He mastered the engineering arts of bridge building and road making. Of special interest were the problems of nutrition for armies on the march, as well as training methods by which green boys from city and farm could be quickly turned into effective soldiers.

By the time José de San Martín was promoted to lieutenant-colonel, he was a real expert at his job. Europe had taught him all she could about war—the practical and theoretical sides to it. He was a master of his profession and was recognized as such in the highest circles of the Spanish officer corps.

But at the same time, the contradiction was growing. As he won prestige and respect for his knowledge and his skill, his unease and discontent with Spain and her goverment, and his ever-increasing identification with the efforts at independence in far off La Plata, also grew. The necessity for making a choice became clear. Was he to be an American, or was he to remain a Spaniard?

As San Martín grappled with this problem and struggled with his conscience, he was not alone. There were many Creoles in Spain. Some were simply traveling, some in business, some in school, and some were low-grade army officers. Proving the logic if not the wisdom of Spain's conviction of the unreliability of these Creoles, almost to a man they were infected with the ideals of freedom for all men and were on fire with dreams of liberty for their native lands.

Many of these Creoles were members of one or another of the many active organizations which advocated freedom for the colonies. These clubs were all subversive, and their members lived in constant fear for their lives, in constant terror of discovery by the monarchy's secret agents.

The foremost and most active of these secret societies was called the Lautaro Society. When the Spanish subdued the Inca empire in South America during the conquests of the early 1500s, they had been unable to conquer one large tribe of Indians who lived far to the south in what is now a part of Chile. This tribe, the Auracanians, are still known today in song and in epic poetry as heroic people who preferred death to submission to oppression. One of their most famous chieftains was named Lautaro, and his name came to symbolize resistance to Spain. The founders of the Lautaro Society used it to symbolize their own unquenchable desire for freedom.

All the activities of the Lautaro Society were, of course, completely underground. Prospective members were observed carefully for long periods of time and thoroughly investigated before being invited to join. No one member ever knew more than the half dozen others in his small group because, if captured, he would inevitably be tortured and forced to talk. Because of this secrecy, very little is known about the Lautaro Society or its inner workings. It is known that it had branches throughout all of Spain, was organized somewhat along the lines of the Masons and had its headquarters in London.

The society smuggled forbidden literature to the colonies, raised money to finance revolts and in general taught the principles and techniques of rebellion to its members. Its principal activity, however, was to recruit soldiers, especially trained and battle-tested officers, and it had long had its eyes on the bronzed and taciturn young Lieutenant-Colonel José de San Martín. No one knows the exact date, but it is thought to have been some-time in 1810, when the leader of the society in Cádiz at last approached him and invited him to join. San Martín was ready; his mind was made up. He accepted the invi-tation and from that time on led a double life—that of a loyal, highly regarded Spanish Army officer, and that of a "traitor," dedicated to the freedom of his homeland.

Nothing whatever is known of San Martín's activities in Spain as a member of the Lautaro Society. It was so secret that later, when the British general Miller asked for information, San Martín replied simply: "I do not consider it fitting to discuss the least detail of the Lodge. . . . These are strictly private matters, and al-though they have exercised and still do exercise great influence in the events of the revolution in that part [Argentina] of America, they could not be revealed without a breach on my part of the most sacred pledges."

During these years, San Martín had his eyes opened as to the absurdity of absolute monarchy as a system of gov-ernment. At the same time, he began to develop a dis-trust in the abilities of the masses of ignorant people to govern themselves! He never forgot the moment when he had to stand by helplessly in Cádiz and watch while a howling mob of so-called free men hacked and stabbed his beloved and very capable commanding officer to death because the general had seemed to hesitate in launching an attack! It became painfully apparent to San Martín that without restraint, personal honor, education and self-discipline, freedom could degenerate into sheer anarchy. Although for the rest of his life he was to battle as a partisan of liberty and political freedom, as time went on his doubts that the "voice of the people was the voice of God" increased. And for him, sadly, throughout all the long years which lay ahead, this question was never truly resolved.

Chapter 3

As THE MOMENTUM OF EVENTS in the Americas picked up speed and reached a critical point, San Martín was like a man poised above an abyss. Treason did not come easily to him. He had already taken the first step—joining the Lautaro Society and allying himself with those who advocated freedom for the colonies. The final step—renouncing openly all that he was, all that Spain had given him, the trust she had reposed in him—awaited. Once this final, public step had been taken, there could be no retreat.

San Martín had a credo by which he lived. It was simple, but it was also terrible in the uncompromising demands it laid upon him. He believed that "one must be what one must, or one will be nothing." As he pondered his dilemma and his decision, he knew what he was and, because of this, what he had to do. He was an American, and he understood finally that he would have to follow this star back to the land of his birth. He decided to put an end to the double life he was leading and return to Argentina to offer his services to the patriots there.

Getting away was not easy; much subterfuge was

necessary. He applied for retirement status from the army and, because of his reputation as a loyal officer, it was granted. The reason that he gave was "for the purpose of going to Peru to take care of family property." The San Martín family was very poor; it had never owned any property in Peru. Nevertheless, the application was accepted without question. Shortly, for the first time in many years, San Martín laid aside his Spanish uniform and donned civilian clothes. He planned to go to London secretly and there join other South Americans who were going home to take up arms in the cause of liberty for their native lands.

A passport was necessary, and it was arranged for him by a close friend, Lord Macduff, who later became the Earl of Fife. Macduff had come to Spain as a simple volunteer to fight with the Spanish against Napoleon, and the two men had met as comrades on the battlefield. With this false passport, and with nothing but the clothes on his back, San Martín journeyed to England. His renunciation was complete; he said nothing to his mother, or to his three brothers, who were still loyal Spanish officers. He never saw any of his family again.

In the first days of January, 1812, San Martín sailed on the British ship *George Canning*. Weeks later the vessel slid with the tide up the estuary of the great La Plata River.

The little band of patriots on her deck watched the city of Buenos Aires rise out of the dissolving morning mists. Included in the group were such young men as Carlos de Alvear and Matias Zapiola, brothers of the Cádiz Lautaro Society, Francisco de Vera, Francisco

Chilabert and a number of others. With them also was a Bavarian, Baron Holmberg, of the Walloon Guards, one of the thousands of Europeans who over the years streamed to the Americas to offer their services to the patriots.

San Martín stood separate from his companions, taking no part in their youthful excitement. He was thirty-four years old; his own youth was long since gone, lost in the bloody disillusionment of the battlefield. Of all those on the ship only he had a true idea of what lay ahead: misery and not glory.

In appearance also, San Martín was far different from the others. Twenty years of campaigning in the open had tanned him so dark that those who knew him well called him *El Indio*—the Indian. He was of medium height, but his body was erect and strong. His eyes were large, nearly jet-black and piercing and his mouth was small but firm and set. He had the unmistakable air of the true military man, the dedicated soldier, sternly self-disciplined and under rigid control at all times, nearly to the point of seeming to reflect disdain at outbursts of emotion or youthful exuberance.

San Martín was somber as he watched Buenos Aires come up on the port bow of the ship. He recognized none of it. To the others, this was home; they were returning after absences in Europe. To San Martín this was an unfamiliar land, his only by right of birth and spiritual affinity.

The tall spires of the great cathedral were pointed out to him by one of his companions. There his mother, Gregoria Matorras, a young Spanish girl, had been married by proxy to her young husband, Juan de San Martín, a lieutenant of infantry who was, at the moment of the wedding, 500 miles away at his post in the north. And off to the starboard side of the ship, barely visible on the shore, was the little village of Montevideo, Uruguay. Beyond it the land sloped gently to the horizon as far as the eye could see. Even farther beyond the horizon, San Martín knew, lay the tiny mission station of Yapeyú, where he had been born. He tried to imagine how his mother must have felt taking off by oxcart across this vast sea of pampas to join her new husband.

All such thoughts were shortly driven from San Martín's mind. The tide was going out, and the *George Canning* rested easily, high and dry on the mudflats. Soon the enormous two-wheeled carts came churning out through the mud to take off cargo and passengers.

When San Martín landed in Buenos Aires, Argentina seemed a lonely outpost at the end of the world. Its people were torn by confusion and disunity and were mortally threatened by the powerful Spanish Army advancing down on them from the north. Already, small advance units were ranging the banks of the La Plata River across from Buenos Aires, feeling out whatever defenses the patriots might have managed to throw together. So enormous was the distance from Peru to Argentina, however, that the main body of these troops was not expected for months. This did not make the threat any less real, but it did give the revolutionaries time to prepare if they could bury their differences and plan for the common defense.

San Martín had come to Argentina, as he said, "to fight for the liberty of my native land," and he lost no time in seeking the opportunity to do so. He immediately offered his services to the *junta,* which was struggling so desperately to organize the nation and prepare for its defense.

At first he was regarded with great suspicion by the *junta* and by other *porteños* who were prominent in the city. To them, this high-ranking army officer was the enemy. To them he was a Spaniard. His years of loyal service, his decorations, his wounds and scars gathered in years of fighting for Spain were not things to inspire confidence in revolutionaries. After all, the only ties, or proofs, pointing to an American background were the marriage records in the cathedral and his own birth in the distant little settlement of Yapeyú. But this had all taken place many years before. His life since then in every respect had been that of a European, a Spaniard. Who could say where his true loyalties were? It was whispered by many that he was a spy.

Nevertheless, San Martín talked sense, and people listened. He alone in the highly charged atmosphere of self-appointed generals and tacticians knew what he was talking about. It soon became obvious that his assessment of the military situation was practical and realistic, far different from the conclusions of the armchair soldiers about him. No one knew better than San Martín the skill of the professional Spanish troops who would oppose the patriots. He was under no illusions about the length of the struggle which lay ahead, or the suffering that would have to be endured. Amateur soldiers would have no chance in such a war, and he said so, coldly and bluntly. He urged the *junta* to prepare for what he knew was surely coming. He urged them to stop talking, to prepare to fight, to start gathering munitions, to work out long-term plans. Above all, he urged that training programs be set up.

The *junta* was finally impressed. San Martín was given the same rank in the infant Argentine Army as he had had in Spain and was authorized to establish a school to train a regiment of mounted grenadiers. The doubts which some still had about his true loyalties quickly vanished as he set to work.

Slavery had been abolished by the Argentine *junta* in 1811, and San Martín was allotted the old slave compound and barracks as a site for his school. There, in the grim old buildings, he settled down and put out the call for recruits. They flocked to him, and the training schedule they found waiting was something new in the happy-go-lucky lives of the young cadets. The undisciplined, highly independent young men—*gauchos, Mestizos* and Creoles—were shocked at the rigors they were asked to endure as they began the hard business of learning to be soldiers.

Gone were the days when military men were little more than gaudily dressed figures whose principal business was to impress the ladies with their dashing skill on a horse. They were ordered to drill and hold exercises all day and study half the night. Finally, worn out by the stern schedule, they tumbled to bed in rude cots, never knowing when they would be routed out to hold night maneuvers.

Most of the young men who came to the school were

already fine horsemen; there was little anyone could have taught them about riding. Nevertheless, they soon discovered there was a vast difference between riding madly over the pampas herding cattle and handling themselves and their mounts as efficient fighting teams.

Beyond such arts, San Martín also insisted that they learn logistics, tactics, engineering, mathematics and all the other basic skills of the military science. In addition to all this, their commanding officer also pounded home the idea of teamwork and cooperation, and the sense that they belonged to an elite and dedicated corps of men, selfless in love of country and liberty. The hard work paid off. The men in these early grenadier squadrons became the nucleus of all the armies which later were to battle the Spanish troops to a finish.

In addition to establishing his school, one of the first things which San Martín did was to set up a branch of the Lautaro Society in Buenos Aires. With several of the brothers from the Cádiz branch, he recruited new members, and soon this branch was a flourishing and powerful, but secret, factor in the entire Argentine revolutionary movement. San Martín was not deeply interested in politics or in the actual processes of organizing and operating a government. He was, however, totally committed to the idea of freedom with responsibility, and it was his firm belief that in young nations, where the populace was ill trained for self-government and where conditions were as chaotic as they were in Argentina at the moment, only societies composed of devoted men, operating behind the scenes, could exercise the influence necessary for stability. Now was not the time, in his opinion, for endless wrangling over the rights of a multitude of small groups, or for arguing over constitutions and the fine points of democracy. Such talking and political skirmishing could come later. A just and strong government should be organized now, and quickly, and to this end he and the other members of the Lautaro Society worked. Desperately hard fighting lay ahead, and if it was to be successful and if the dreams of the patriots were to come true, then a stable government was badly needed to back up the armed forces.

With San Martín and the Lautaro Society quietly providing the leadership and giving inspiration and advice, a working government was established. The animosities between various quarreling factions were buried, at least for the moment, and the nation settled down as best it could to work as a unit. At this time also, the people of Argentina took the final plunge of making a formal declaration of freedom from Spain and laying plans for the fighting which lay ahead in order to make it a reality.

Another matter claimed San Martín's attention during these early months in Buenos Aires. The city boasted a full and very active social life, patterned after the French style and centered about the salons of the town's big and elegant homes. Naturally, during such times, a great deal of the conversation had to do with plots and counterplots, revolution and politics. There was also dancing, light talk and much good food. The atmosphere combined the rustic and patriarchal simplicity of the old colonial families with the formal manner of the Spanish Viceroys.

Although since the age of eleven San Martín's only home had been the barracks and the bivouac, his manner was not that of a rough soldier. He had a natural courtliness and grace, and somewhere he had learned to be an excellent dancer. His voice was grave, deep and masculine, and he was an excellent conversationalist. He didn't speak with the affected mannerisms of so many of his contemporaries, but rather with the direct simplicity and pithy accuracy he had learned from simple soldiers. San Martín didn't talk at great length, but when he spoke he did so with eloquence and to the point.

Such a figure was bound to be a commanding one in Buenos Aires, and he was much in demand in the various salons. One of the most elegant drawing rooms to which he was welcomed was that of Don Antonio José de Escalada, a rich and influential Creole who wholeheartedly backed the cause of independence. San Martín was often to be found in this house, expressing his views and trying to influence other men he met there. But politics and government were not the only reason he frequented the Escalada household.

Old Don Antonio had two daughters. Both were lovely, but one of them, a girl not yet sixteen years of age, was exquisite. Her name was María de Remedios, and she fell completely in love with the tall soldier who had given up his career in Spain and come from so far across the sea to fight for the freedom of his homeland. Five months after his arrival in Buenos Aires, they were married. Remeditos, as he called her, became the faithful companion of his life. Even though the fates of war were to keep them cruelly separated for long periods, the young girl, little more than a child bride, remained the devoted wife of the man she loved.

But José de San Martín had not returned to the New World to dedicate himself to the role of the doting husband any more than he had come to devote himself to politics. He had come as a soldier. In January, 1813, just a few months after his marriage, he was to prove to his countrymen how excellent a fighting man he was and the value of the training he had insisted upon for his grenadiers.

The *junta* had managed to clean out most of the diehard monarchists and royalist troops on the Buenos Aires side of the La Plata River. These people had escaped across the enormously wide estuary to find refuge on the opposite bank, in and around the city of Montevideo. There they were besieged by patriot forces, but they had a considerable number of strong naval ships at their disposal and were able to range up and down the river, pillaging, burning and terrorizing the helpless and unorganized country people.

Some miles up the La Plata from Buenos Aires, just above the point where it divides into the Uruguay and Paraná Rivers, lay the little town of San Lorenzo. There the Paraná was very wide and slow-moving, the village and the countryside peaceful and quiet.

Early on the morning of February 3, 1813, a powerful Spanish fleet of eleven vessels crept over the burnished silver waters toward the shore. The purpose of the force was to collect provisions, cut the trade routes from Buenos Aires to the interior and establish a bridgehead on the south bank, from which an all-out attack on Argentina could be launched at a later date.

A Franciscan monastery in San Lorenzo with a tall church spire on its chapel offered a sweeping view of the river and shoreline. From this commanding vantage point San Martín watched and waited. Below him was a strong contingent of his grenadiers, also hidden from view and waiting. They had ridden hard all night long in order to arrive in time to oppose the landing.

The enemy fleet finally anchored in the lee of large bluffs below the town. Heavily armed soldiers and marines immediately disembarked in small boats. Their equipment included four small but powerful assault cannon, which were dragged ashore and emplaced.

Carefully San Martín observed the enemy as they set up weapons and formed up for the movement inland. He wanted to catch them at precisely the right moment. With San Martín was a friend, an English merchant named William Robertson. He had known Robertson in Buenos Aires and had permitted him to accompany the detachment to observe the action. He insisted, however, on giving Robertson a good horse, with the warning: "Your duty is not to fight; if the battle goes against us, you are to run to safety."

Slowly the Spanish advanced. Already the day was burning hot. San Martín remarked to Robertson, "In two more minutes we shall be upon them."

He then descended from the tower to join his men and to go over the battle plan with his lieutenants once more. This was to be no helter-skelter attack by brave but disorganized men. It was to be a highly disciplined maneuver, tightly controlled, with all possible adverse contingencies covered in advance.

In a last-minute conference with his second-in-command, San Martín repeated the basic plan for the attack. "Remember," he said, "control your men. Do not attack at random. We shall attack in two columns, in two halves, one on each side. In the center of the enemy column we shall meet, and according to the way the battle has developed, I shall give you further orders."

With this San Martín drew his sword, gave the order to advance to his bugler, spurred his horse and personally led one of the columns. In an instant they were met by furious and determined fire from the Spanish small arms and the cannon. The two bodies of men—one mounted and the other on foot—met with a clash. Over the peaceful river rose the battle cries "Long live our king!" And "Long live our country!"

As San Martín had well known—he had fought beside such soldiers many times in his life—the Spanish did not break or throw down their arms. They stood and fought as they had been trained to do, with courage and skill. No quarter was asked or given. The struggle was long and desperately fought by both sides. San Martín was in the thick of it; his horse was killed, shot out from under him by a bursting shell. As the infantry bayonets came in for the kill, his life was saved by one of his sergeants, Juan Batista Cabral, who was mortally wounded in the action and died two hours later.

As though it was a preview of the warfare and bloodletting which lay ahead, this preliminary encounter was savage and deadly. In the wild, hand-to-hand conflict which developed before the invaders were finally able to fight their way back to the safety of their ships, they lost forty dead and more than 200 wounded out of their entire force of 300 men. The grenadiers lost fifteen dead and twenty-seven wounded.

Although the battle of San Lorenzo was small in terms of the number of men involved, it was a very important engagement. It cleared the river of the fierce foraging attacks by the Spanish and led to the ultimate capture of Montevideo by the patriots. Far more than this, it boosted the morale of the people of Argentina. It was Argentina's first victory as an independent nation—something badly needed.

San Martín was the hero of the moment, acclaimed as the savior of the country. It was the beginning of his rise as one of the real leaders of the nation. Gone was the talk of his possible loyalty to Spain. He was feted from one end of Buenos Aires to the other, entrusted with the defenses of the city and ordered by the heartened *junta* to prepare plans for the continuance of the war.

Chapter 4

THE PERIOD AFTER THE BATTLE of San Lorenzo was a time of triumph for José de San Martín. It was also a time for his real immersion into the confusion of Latin-American politics, a time when his eyes were finally and fully opened to the profound depths of the chaos which was to accompany every single effort made on the continent to establish free and workable governments. This confusion was no worse in Argentina than it was in the other nations as they became free, but it was in Argentina that San Martín first became truly aware of the problems that lay ahead. He had had intimations of this, but only after the battle of San Lorenzo did the patterns become crystal clear.

As fast as one group of politicians managed to get enough power together to have a chance of governing effectively, it would degenerate into quarreling, bickering factions, at odds with each other and at odds with all those outside it. Each of these factions followed a leader, or *caudillo*. Nothing could ever be agreed upon. No compromise was ever possible, as each man and his faction considered their own plan to be the best of all possible

51

plans. In the confusion, democracy, which can exist only in a spirit of mutual give and take, was of course lost, and the stage was set for rule by force.

There were many causes for this chaotic state of affairs. One of the most important was the fact that for centuries the people of Spain's colonies had had absolutely no training in even the rudiments of self-government. Spain's intent had been to keep them as children, and she had succeeded. The Spanish had at least *governed,* although not too well and with little interest in the lands and peoples they ruled. When they were gone, the restraints were removed. Self-restraint and self-discipline were unknown qualities. Without the externally imposed restraints, the people were lost. When the responsibilities of government fell on the Creoles, they simply were unable to unite in common cause and put love of country ahead of their own interests. To complicate this, there were enormous numbers of Creoles, *Mestizos* and Indians without education of any kind whatsoever. These people could be wooed and swayed by whatever politician promised them the most, or talked most convincingly of their rights.

Always simmering, this political pot's temperature rose to a running boil after the battle of San Lorenzo. Argentina was free now, or so it seemed to the enterprising and self-seeking politicians, and they made the most of it. In spite of San Martín's popularity, they began to eye him warily. He was too popular; he was, in their eyes, getting too much power. His Spanish European background was brought up again, his motives questioned. They could not comprehend that he was as he insisted: absolutely without personal ambition and motivated only by love of freedom and love for his native land. Thus San Martín was caught up in the broils of far inferior men, a predicament which he was helpless to combat and which was to bring him much misery for the rest of his life.

Nevertheless, San Martín put his growing unease and dissatisfaction with the government behind him. He knew that the fight for freedom had not yet even commenced and that there was much work still to be done.

Royalist forces from Peru continued to be a grave threat in the north. The *junta* army fighting them, commanded by General Manuel Belgrano, won several victories, but was terribly mauled and defeated by the Spanish in October of 1813 at the battle of Vilcapugio. In November of the same year, it was routed and practically dispersed on the plains of Ayohuma.

General Belgrano was a man of the very highest personal integrity and honor, but far too kindly and lenient, considering the savagery of the war he was called upon to fight. For example, after one victory he set 3,000 royalist prisoners free, simply accepting their word that they would never take up arms against Argentina again. Naturally, they promptly rejoined the royalist forces, were rearmed and continued to fight.

Belgrano was a school teacher; war was not his profession. After one of his victories a grateful National Assembly awarded him a present of 40,000 pesos and he insisted that the money be used to build schools. He and San Martín had been in close correspondence, and in one of his letters he humbly confessed, "Because God has so willed I find myself being a general without knowing what I am about. This has not been my career. . . . I have no one to help me. . . . I make war like an explorer without a single officer who can claim professional knowledge. . . ."

Belgrano was anxious to meet San Martín. He was convinced that only a truly professional military man could possibly bring victory to the patriots. Their friendship, based on respect, trust and confidence, lasted for years.

The clique in power in Buenos Aires decided the time had come to get San Martín out of the city. He was far too popular for their tastes. So, ostensibly to relieve Belgrano for having failed in battle, they sent San Martín north to take his place. He kissed his young bride farewell and set out on the long journey.

He and Belgrano met early in 1814, and liked each other immediately. They found something in each other that put them far above the petty bickering going on around them. Belgrano opened his heart to San Martín and told him, "You must not only be my friend, but my teacher and my companion and chief if you wish to be." These were indeed unusual words from a man who was being relieved in "disgrace" to his replacement.

San Martín reciprocated such candor, and he later wrote: ". . . He is the most methodical man of all whom I know in America; he is full of integrity and natural talent. He may not have the military knowledge of a Moreau or a Bonaparte so far as the army is concerned, but believe me, he is the best we have in South America."

The exchange of command took place on January 30, 1814. As he took over the army of the north, San Martín wrote, "I have found only the sad fragments of a beaten army. . . . No medical care . . . half-naked troops, dressed like beggars . . . a thousand clamorings for overdue pay. . . ."

However, he set to work to do what had to be done: to build, train and equip an army. With a nucleus of trained grenadiers sent up from the school in Buenos Aires, schools for the officers and men were established and munitions were accumulated. Eventually, San Martín felt strong enough to risk contact with the enemy. After a series of short but extremely bloody battles, the Spanish reconquest of Argentina ground to a temporary halt.

By the end of 1814 the military situation was sufficiently under control for San Martín to have time to breathe freely and rest a bit. He needed the rest, for he was ill. The gastric ulcers from which he suffered were beginning to flare up badly. He was starting to hemorrhage, and the pain was continual. More and more he was relying on heavy doses of opiates for relief.

But even more pressing than the need for physical rest, San Martín wanted the time and tranquility to work out certain long-range plans in his mind. By now he had had the opportunity to look very hard and carefully at the course which the war would take. His conclusion was that the fighting which was going on now was not the real fight, nor would it ever be, in spite of appearances and in spite of its momentary immediate importance.

The bastion of Spanish power in South America was Peru. Here was the real threat. Until Spanish strength there had been crushed there could be no such thing as lasting independence for La Plata, or anywhere else on the continent. With the unerring vision of the true strategist, San Martín saw the struggle in its broadest aspects. It was continental, no matter how vital small local engagements might seem to be. Unless these smaller engagements could be integrated into a larger plan, they were simply encounters which in the long run would have little effect other than to drain away patriot strength. The problem of winning the war had to be considered on a vaster scale.

The passes through the jungles and deserts and immense mountains in the north did not offer an effective route for Spanish troops in Peru to cross over and subdue La Plata. For the same reasons, this route could never be an effective way for Argentine troops to invade Peru. A lifetime involvement in military matters had taught San Martín what armies could do and what they could not do. He knew without a shadow of a doubt that neither force could ever bring enough power to bear on the enemy to reach a conclusive victory. The war for each side would never amount to more than a series of holding actions and sharp skirmishes. Troops certainly would have to be kept in the area, but their purpose would primarily be to harass the enemy and force him to pin down soldiers who might better be used elsewhere.

For months San Martín pored over such maps as he had until the whole immense continent seemed to unfold before him and to become one enormous battlefield. In these terms he grasped its military secrets, and unerringly he reached his conclusions. When his mind was made up, he wrote simply, "The route to Peru is not here, but across the mountains in the south into Chile." But how was this to be organized, to be accomplished? There was not so much as one soldier or one spare cannon for such a campaign. Methodically he made his plans. First things first.

For reasons of his health, he requested that he be relieved of his command and appointed governor of the inland province of Cuyo, far to the southwest. He gave no other reason for the request. Plans laid on so vast a scale had to be kept secret. The government must have been shocked at the request of its best general to be relieved from what seemed to be a terribly dangerous military situation, but they gave in to him. After all, the times were so confused that just about anything could seem reasonable.

San Martín let one aspect of his plans slip out. He convinced the government that an invasion of Peru from the north was impossible, and he persuaded it to adopt a purely defensive position. The forces for this he entrusted to his most capable lieutenant, General Martín de Güimes. For years General de Güimes and his hard-riding *gaucho* cavalry kept up a devastating war of harassment against the Spanish on this front. This had exactly the effect San Martín desired; it took attention away from himself and his own work, protected Argentina's northern frontier and forced the enemy to keep considerable numbers of troops in the area.

Late in the fall of 1814, San Martín made the long journey to Mendoza, the capital of the province of Cuyo. It was only some 200-odd miles from Mendoza to the Pacific Ocean, but the enormous bulk of the Andes rose to the clouds between the town and the sea. Through the icy passes threading these soaring peaks, San Martín proposed to lead his as yet nonexistent army

to distant Peru. This was his "back door," the way to
Peru which he proposed to keep secret as long as possible.

While in the far northern part of the continent, Simón
Bolívar rushed valiantly and headlong into a hundred
fruitless and disastrous battles at the head of ragged
troops, in the south, San Martín did just the opposite.
Bolívar did not start out as a soldier. He learned his trade
the hard way as he went along, and he needed many years
to discover that the first thing to do in fighting a war is
to prepare for it. San Martín had learned his lessons years
before, and he did not fall into the fatal trap of prema-
ture action. He settled down in Mendoza to begin the
long and difficult task of building a modern army.

The job of building the "Army of the Andes," as it
eventually was to be called, took nearly three years. In a
life which was spent for the most part in a rough, hard
world, these years were the happiest which San Martín
was ever to know. In spite of endless trials and hard work,
the days in Mendoza were those dearest to his heart. "Oh
rare and happy Mendoza," he wrote, "here reigns tranquil
peace."

Mendoza lies about 800 miles inland from the Atlantic,
in the foothills of the Andes. To the east, like a boundless ocean, stretch the waving grasses of the pampas. It is
a land of sunshine, of flowers, vineyards and fruit, well
irrigated and carefully tended by those who live there. Its
long irrigation canals, even in San Martín's time, were
lined with graceful poplars, swaying in the wind and cast-
ing long shadows across the sunny, fertile fields. It was a
land of well-being and abundance.

One of the first things which San Martín did after he settled down in Mendoza was to send to Buenos Aires for Remedios. In nearly two years of marriage, he and his wife had been together only a few months. Like his own mother so many years before, Remedios left her home and parents in Buenos Aires to join her husband.

Of all places on land, the pampas most closely give the illusion of the sea. Perfectly flat, they stretch level and unbroken for hundreds upon hundreds of miles in all directions. The tall grasses undulate softly in the wind like the waves and swells of the ocean. Great flocks of white-breasted gulls—true sea-birds that long ago migrated from thcir natural abode and established themselves on this sea of earth—complete the illusion of a marine world. Except for foreign trees which have been imported and planted around ranch buildings, hostels, and other dwellings, there are no trees on the pampas with the exception of the ombu. Ombus only grow at very rare intervals, and their fantastic knotted trunks and enormous leafy branches can be seen for miles. In a world as trackless and devoid of landmarks as these plains, it is entirely fitting that travelers set their courses by the ombus, and that they are known as "the lighthouses of the pampas."

Remedios and the people who accompanied her on her long trip traveled on horseback and in *carretas*. In legend and in song, *carretas* occupy the same place in the lore of this part of the world as do the covered wagons, the "prairie schooners" of the early days in the west of our own country. *Carretas*, known as "ships of the pampas," were not wagons, but enormous, covered, two-wheeled carts. They carried tremendous loads and were famous for the great size of their wheels, which sometimes measured as much as eight feet in diameter. This large size enabled them to move safely through deep mud and across streams. They were usually drawn by six or eight oxen, with the lead pair strung out a long distance ahead. This lead pair could cross bogs and mud holes to dry land and then help pull the others across.

Carretas generally traveled in trains of fifteen or twenty, heavily protected by armed outriders who ranged widely through the country on each side. Now and again, the lurching, creaking carts passed another train bound for Buenos Aires, loaded with wines, hides and other products of the interior. Occasionally squadrons of gauchos went by the train, eyeing Remedios and her company greedily and with menace, and were just as suspiciously eyed by the guards. They rolled past on their horses, swaying easily in the saddles, and vanished into the horizon as fleets pass each other and vanish on the sea. At other times, lone Indians or gauchos would whirl by, bolados swinging wildly, in hot pursuit of ostriches. (Bolados are the lassoos of the pampas and consist of long strips of rawhide with rocks tied to their ends. When sent spinning after an ostrich, or perhaps a fleeing man or steer, they wrap themselves around the legs of their prey and bring it to earth, unfortunately often breaking the legs of the creature in the process.) Other than occasional ostriches, there were few animals or natural life of any kind except birds. The pampas were empty.

Time passed slowly for Remedios and her people. Now and then a lonely ranch estancia gave them refuge for a night. Occasionally there was a rude frontier hotel or way house. Most of the time, however, they were on their own, camping and sleeping under the stars. At this time Remedios was eighteen years old. Her life had been easy and highly protected, as were the lives of all well-born young ladies of those days. The journey was long—*carretas* traveled only fifteen or twenty miles a day—and it must have been wearying for her, and terrifying in some ways, but wonderfully interesting in others.

At long last the trip was over, and Remedios was greeted by San Martín in Mendoza. He had been offered the governor's mansion but had turned it down. He envisioned the years ahead as filled with hard work, frugality and discipline and intended that the life which he and his wife were to live would be an example for everyone— simple and without ostentation. He and "Remeditos," as he called her, settled down in a modest cottage where they could live simply. It was a happy time for them, the only time in their lives when they truly lived together. War was to come between them always, but here and now it seemed far away. San Martín lived as he wished to live, content and in peace. Here in Mendoza also, their only child was born in 1816. The little daughter, christened Mercedes Tomasa, in later years became her father's strong right arm.

The small house of the San Martíns' became a center for much of the social life of Mendoza. Remedios was a cheerful, happy young girl, very much in love with her husband, and her joy at being with him was infectious. She organized her home for him and made it a haven of contentment and rest, as well as a place where the people who slowly began streaming to Mendoza from all of

South America could become acquainted and get to know each other on a level apart from the hard military world where they worked. There were parties and dances in the little house which were particularly appreciated by the young officers, who were lonely and far from home. Here they could relax and, what was even more important, meet the young *señoritas* and belles of the province. San Martín's life and profession had of necessity taken him from the world and its lighter pleasures, but in the warm glow of joyousness spread by his young wife, he unbent and relaxed.

Like so many great men, San Martín had a deep and abiding love for the fruitful earth. Among the many reasons why he had chosen this small cottage for himself and Remedios was that there was a bit of open ground around it, and he could indulge his passion for gardening.

He had his eye on more land, however. There was nothing he wanted more than to own a bit of this rich and beautiful Mendoza earth for himself. To buy it was out of the question. He had no money and, because he had voluntarily relinquished half of the small salary he was paid, lived a life of near penury. The urge to own some land was overpowering, however. After much thought, he decided to petition the government of the town to award the small piece he had his eye on as a gift. He wrote humbly to the town fathers, saying in part: "It is very natural for a man to think of the conditions in which he plans to spend the tired years of his old age. The condition of a farmer is one that I feel to be my nature, and as a resource and a refuge against the worries of my whole life, which I have devoted to the army. . . ."

He went on to discuss the small farm which he found and liked, and ended with: ". . . That is to say, the fifty squares which I ask as a gift are worth only about two hundred pesos. I have not got this amount; if I had it I would buy it myself."

To the everlasting credit of the government of Mendoza, the land was presented free to San Martín. Nearly 200 squares more were given to his little daughter, Mercedes. San Martín declined this gift and suggested that it be used instead for officers who would be wounded or distinguish themselves in the fighting which lay ahead.

The government council overruled this suggestion, replying that parents had no right to make a decision which would be to the detriment of their minor children. They insisted that the land be registered and maintained in the name of the infant girl. Another 200-square piece was purchased and set aside for the use of future officer veterans who might need it.

And so it was. Great general though he might be, even San Martín could not expect to win every battle.

Chapter 5

MEANTIME, IN THE MIDST of such pleasant activities, the task of building the Army of the Andes slipped into high gear. This was an army created out of hopes and dreams; if ever a fighting force rose up out of nothing, it was this one.

San Martín's dedication was pervasive and catching. As the dream of the Army of the Andes began to take life and substance, its demands came to dominate every aspect of life in Mendoza and the surrounding areas.

Remedios was as busy as her husband in preparing for war. She organized the ladies in a wide variety of projects. Cheerfully they turned in all their jewels—diamonds, necklaces, beautifully made gold pieces, priceless heirlooms from the days of the *conquistadores*—and ordered them sold to pay for sabers, muskets and shot. They stitched and hemmed banners and pennants. Groups were organized to card and spin and weave the heavy wool of the countryside into cloth, which was dyed blue and then cut into uniforms for the men. Remedios was at the head of all such activities, and in a thousand ways she proved herself worthy of her husband.

The citizens of Mendoza and those of the cities in the surrounding provinces came to consider themselves involved in a cause that was almost holy. To a man, down to the smallest children, San Martín's dream of defeating the Spanish through this campaign across the Andes became their dream. In numberless ways they responded to the quiet magic and enthusiasm of the general and pitched in to make this war their war. Farmers contributed food to feed the growing battalions of soldiers. A handful of English residents in the area banded themselves into a medical unit and began accumulating tents, bandages, medicines and other supplies. The slaves in the area were granted freedom by their owners, and more than 700 organized into an all-Negro battalion and presented themselves to San Martín for training. It is indeed worth mentioning that these blacks fought with great valor and distinction through the years of war ahead—so much so that all but a handful sacrificed their lives to the cause of independence.

Regardless of all the help and enthusiasm and goodwill of the people of the area, many of the items needed by the growing army were hard to come by in Mendoza. Not all the requirements were as simple as homemade uniforms, banners, flags and free food for recruits. Hard munitions were another thing. For them, money was needed, and at first, particularly, there was never enough of it. In the early part of the struggle to build an army, San Martín and Mendoza were nearly alone.

This lack of help was due to a number of reasons, but it was mainly because few people outside of Mendoza knew what San Martín was up to. Even had they known, without his grasp of the wider strategy of the war, they possibly wouldn't have approved. And this secrecy was absolutely necessary in order to keep the Spanish in the dark as long as possible. It seems incredible, but for a year and a half, the plans *were* kept secret. A very efficient counterintelligence system was developed with the purpose of seeing to it that the enemy received a steady stream of "captured" documents especially prepared to deceive them.

One day, a strange-looking and eccentric Franciscan friar named Father Luis Beltran arrived in Mendoza. San Martín heard of the odd qualities of this person and visited him where he was praying. After a brief talk San Martín was convinced that this man was exactly what he needed and persuaded him to come out into the world to assist the war effort.

Father Luis was a "do-it-yourself" expert, a kind of South American Leonardo da Vinci. He had an absolute genius for designing or operating any mechanical device, or for working out the production details for any technical process. As a young officer, San Martín for years had studied the scientific aspects of the production of munitions. He knew a great deal about the subject, but even he was startled at the depths of Father Luis' knowledge. According to him, the good *padre* soon became the mainspring of the entire effort to arm.

What the priest accomplished is truly amazing. He turned Mendoza into a humming center for the production of the muscles of war, using mainly the materials at hand. An arsenal was set up for the manufacture of gunpowder. Shops were built to repair old or damaged muskets. The forges turned out 50,000 horseshoes as well as thousands of lances and sabers. No metal available for canteens? Father Luis designed a way to seal up the horns of cattle and make them into serviceable containers to carry the water the soldiers would need. Heavy bronze and brass bells were lowered from church towers, melted down and recast into cannon. Knapsacks, bandoliers for ammunition, shoes, saddles and harnesses were made, as well as special portable gun carriages and gun sleds which could be dismantled and taken piece by piece over difficult mountain trails.

Father Luis and San Martín got along famously, as might have been expected. As the priest said, "If General San Martín wants wings on his cannons to fly them across the Andean gorges, he shall have them." Failing in the production of wings, Father Luis took a leaf from the Andean Inca engineers of ancient times. He spun great fiber cables for suspension bridges which were strong enough to transport huge weights across the chasms which the army would have to cross.

San Martín had always been interested in the problem of nutrition for armies on the move. Now he and Father Luis concocted a portable ration, a sort of "C" ration, which consisted of dried beef ground to a powder, then mixed with salt, pepper, fats and dried onions. Such a food was extremely nourishing, would keep without spoiling and was so compact that a soldier could easily carry many days' supply with him.

As this capable priest, the long skirts of his habit rolled up and flapping, bustled so efficiently about Mendoza, San Martín was able to devote much more time to training and to planning. Again, as he always had in the past, he insisted that the recruits be painstakingly taught the techniques which would turn them into effective soldiers. Without this knowledge they would only lose battles and be helplessly slaughtered, regardless of their bravery or of the righteousness of their cause. He was helped immeasurably in the task of training by the arrival of hundreds of men and officers from the grenadier cavalry squadrons he had trained in Buenos Aires. Their presence was invaluable, for they were thoroughly trained, and most of them had been battle-tested on the northern front as well. These veterans became the nucleus about which the Army of the Andes was built, and under their steadying influence discipline among the recruits improved and their sense of responsibility and teamwork was strengthened. Slowly the disorganized cadres began turning into reliable fighting units.

Another event took place during these years which was a mixed blessing for San Martín. In one way it increased the difficulties of the tasks which lay ahead; in another it contributed greatly to the gathering strength of the army.

Of all the fantastic stories played out in the enormous lands of the Spanish colonies in America, none is wilder or more improbable than the story of the O'Higgins family in Chile.

Ambrose O'Higgins was a poor country lad, a kitchen scullion in a great medieval manor castle in the southern part of Ireland. He was no ordinary country bumpkin, however. Little Ambrose had wit, courage, intelligence and an overpowering curiosity about foreign lands and places. He was also a devout Roman Catholic, and he wanted with all his heart to become a priest. A kindly uncle sent the youngster to Spain, and after years in a seminary there, he was graduated, ordained and sent to the New World to fill out his vocation. He arrived in Buenos Aires about 1770, but he soon found he was not cut out for the humdrum tranquility of the life of a parish priest. Bigger, more exciting things were clamoring than counseling the poor or listening to the confessions of staid *señoras*. A whole virgin continent was beyond the horizon of the pampas, and its call was irresistible.

He renounced the priesthood, gave up his life as a *padre* and headed westward into the mountains, plains and jungles. Before his life was done Ambrose O'Higgins played out as fabulous a story of adventure as that of any buccaneer on the Spanish Main.

First he rounded up a handful of *Mestizo* and Indian helpers, all as restless and untamed as he, and then, with a packtrain of a few mules, set himself up as an itinerant peddler in the vast back-country of Argentina, Peru and Chile. For several years he roamed the wide spaces, from dizzy Andean trails to dripping jungle tunnels, selling calico, needles, thread, mirrors, beads, powder, lead and whatever other items people living in remote places were likely to need.

O'Higgins had a quick Irish wit and a capacity for backbreaking work. He also had a very fast eye for profits, and he prospered. Eventually he acquired land and wealth far beyond his wildest dreams. He also acquired something else: a towering reputation as a man of his word, a man of fairness and of scrupulous honesty. This was no small thing in a land where dishonesty, self-interest and laziness were the rule among people who devoted most of their energies to scheming for royal favors and grants.

Finally, the King of Spain appointed "Father Ambrose" —it was *Don Ambrosio* now—governor of the Captaincy-General of Chile, a part of Peru. As governor, he accomplished much. He modernized outmoded agricultural methods and brought in new products which flourished in Chile's fertile soil and widely varied climates. He built schools, roads, harbors and fortifications and pacified still warring tribes of Indians. He did so well and served the king so loyally that he was appointed Viceroy of Peru itself, the only case known where a non-Spaniard occupied such an exalted post. He went to live in the grand royal palace in Pizarro's "City of Kings," Lima.

Not the least of Don Ambrosio's accomplishments was to produce a son by his Chilean wife. The little boy was given a good Irish name—Bernardo O'Higgins—and sent as a child to England for an education. Don Ambrosio believed in education. He had high hopes for his son and had no intention of letting him grow up in idleness and ignorance, in the way of so many other young Creoles, whose main accomplishments were dancing, flirting, guitar playing and horseback riding.

Young Bernardo O'Higgins spent many years in Europe, absorbing the latest heresies of liberal thought. On his trips home to South America, he was appalled at the backwardness, poverty, inequality and ignorance. He began to see clearly that none of these things would ever change until Chile had freed herself from her tyrannical motherland—Spain. Like many other young Creoles in Europe, he became an avowed enemy of the monarchy of Spain and implacable advocate of freedom for the colonies.

Bernardo O'Higgins—he was *Don Bernardo* now—took the final step in London and joined the Lautaro Society. Here he met and plotted and talked endlessly with other "hotheads," such as Simón Bolívar and Francisco de Miranda, who were already planning to lead a force to start the fight for the liberation of Venezuela.

Also, in Cadiz, Bernardo O'Higgins met another young man, a Lautaro brother. He was a battle-scarred Spanish Army officer named José de San Martín. The two young men did not become close. Identities were guarded, and friendships did not go beyond the most casual contact. They met briefly and then went their different ways. They were to meet again, however, years later, and this time their friendship and trust in each other became a deep and abiding bond.

The movement for independence in Chile burst into violent revolution in September of 1810, a few months later than the movement in Buenos Aires. Don Bernardo O'Higgins was in the forefront of the group of young revolutionaries who led the revolt.

For a time all went well. The Spanish Governor was forced to resign. A congress was elected, and steps were taken to put a liberal, democratic government in operation. Seaports were opened to unrestricted free trade, slavery was abolished and many other long-overdue reforms were put in effect.

Nevertheless, Chile was not immune to the common

Spanish-American disease of quarreling disunity. When the break was finally made, and formal independence did away with the fiction that the *junta*-type government was merely running the country in "trust" for King Ferdinand, the divided loyalties and ambitions of the people quickly drove the nation into open civil war. On one side were the violent young Creoles, who would accept nothing less than complete independence. On the other were the *Peninsulares* and the wealthy, conservative Creole families, who wanted nothing so much as a return to the old monarchal ways. On top of this, the young liberal patriots themselves could agree on nothing. They bickered and quarreled and allowed their strength to ebb away in eternal, angry debate.

In spite of all this, the patriots managed to hold their own and were making real progress in putting down the civil war and setting up a good, workable government. Then, in 1814, the defeat of the Argentine *junta*'s army on the northern front freed thousands of Spanish troops for duty elsewhere, exactly as San Martín had predicted. These soldiers were promptly sent to Chile to quell the revolt there. In the face of this mortal peril the Chilean patriots managed to stop quarreling and put up a common front. By then it was too late. They were outnumbered five to one and were disastrously defeated at the battle of Roncagua in October of 1814. Reprisals were savage, and the earth of Chile ran red with blood as the monarchists taught the patriots a lesson they would not soon forget.

The collapse of independent Chile immediately complicated matters for San Martín. He knew that his ultimate goal, Peru, would be fiercely defended. Now, however, instead of having just this one war on his hands, he had two. Chile would first have to be reconquered and the Spaniards there subdued before any plans could be made to continue on into Peru.

This added burden was considerably lessened by the arrival of Chilean soldiers who had survived their defeat and the subsequent bloodbath. By ones and twos and by the hundreds they made their way across the Andes to swell San Martín's army in Mendoza. These men were priceless, all of them veterans with years of experience fighting the Spanish. They asked nothing more than to be given arms and the opportunity to fight once again for the freedom of their homeland.

Among these refugee soldiers and patriots was Bernardo O'Higgins. The previous, casual relationship between him and San Martín bloomed into real friendship. O'Higgins became San Martín's trusted right hand and a passionate believer in the plan to oust the Spanish from Peru through the back-door invasion route over the Andes.

San Martín was surrounded by eager, hard-working people, all of them desperately trying to be of assistance. In spite of this, however, he labored virtually alone. He was the only professional and battle-experienced leader, and it was upon him that the cares and the decisions ultimately descended—from those involving sophisticated military matters and the largest concepts of strategy right down to the thousands and thousands of small details. His was a task which would have crushed a lesser man; and as time went on these burdens increased by matters over which he had absolutely no control.

Napoleon was defeated at Waterloo in June of 1815. The nations of Europe struggled to rise up out of the ruins of twenty-five years of warfare, and the principal instrument for this purpose was an organization known as the Holy Alliance. Semipolitical, semireligious, its purpose was to make the world once again safe for monarchy. The chief members of the alliance were Russia, Austria and Prussia, and their basic tenet was that rule by kings was indeed sanctioned by God and that self-government was only a temporary sickness which had inflamed the minds of the common people. The chief statesman and architect of this infamous alliance was an Austrian— Prince Klemens von Metternich. He resolutely set to work putting kings securely back on their thrones and, by means of force, torture and oppression, doing everything possible to destroy the idea of rule by democratic processes.

One of the first acts of the Holy Alliance was to reinstall the nearly imbecilic "good King Ferdinand" back on the throne of Spain. King Ferdinand knew exactly what was expected of him.

Spain was filled with experienced and hard-bitten veterans of the recent wars, and Ferdinand and his advisers lost no time putting them to work. Powerful forces sailed immediately for the New World to put down the fires of rebellion, with even larger numbers of troops destined to sail as soon as they could be transported. The

Spanish monarchy was determined to crush the revolts of its disloyal subjects for once and for all.

San Martín's heart must have sunk when he learned the names of the generals who commanded these troops: General de la Serna, General Pezuela, General Pablo Morillo and others, the flower of the Spanish Officer Corps. He knew them; he had fought with them. And he also knew the caliber of the men they led. Here were no soft colonials with wavering loyalties, no inexperienced *Mestizos,* blacks or Indians. Instead, they were superbly armed, loyal veterans of hundreds of battles across half of Europe.

The bad news was not long in coming. By the end of 1815, and into the early part of 1816, patriot forces from Mexico to Venezuela found themselves outmatched. They were on the run everywhere, literally fleeing for their lives. In November, 1815, once again the struggling Argentine *junta* armies in the north were soundly and devastatingly trounced at the very spot where a year and a half before San Martín had said they must conduct a holding operation only. Instead, they had tried to "invade" and had been pounced upon by the wily General Pezuela. Spanish historians of the day gleefully announced that with this defeat, "the revolution in La Plata had been beheaded."

Consternation in the colonies was widespread. The feeling was that the cause of freedom was truly lost. The Spanish now moved nearly all their troops from Argentina's northern border to Chile and massed them with those there already to await the Army of the Andes. More ominous than this, reports began coming to San Martín that the Spanish were planning to cross the Andes from Chile to Mendoza to attack San Martín's half-prepared army.

San Martín was a realist. He was under no illusions as to the abilities of his old companions who commanded the royalists. He knew full well that if *he* could plan to cross the mountains from Mendoza to Chile, then *they* could most certainly cross the mountains from Chile to Mendoza. For resolute men the mountain passes ran both ways.

Late in 1816 this invasion seemed imminent. In Mendoza there was no time now for anything but war, and the orders were "Hurry, hurry, hurry." Clearly he outlined the situation in a proclamation: "The moment is near when, the snows of the cordillera that separates us from Chile having melted, the danger of invasion will be present. . . . Prepare yourselves for new sacrifices to avoid that risk. . . . It is for you to win the war and gain a permanent peace. I make bold to predict it, counting upon your help, under the protection of heaven, which looks with horror upon the unjust cause of America's oppressors."

The situation could not have been more sinister. The Spanish possibly were planning to invade Mendoza and fall upon the half-ready troops there. And even if they did not, even if they simply elected to wait in Chile for the Army of the Andes as it emerged from the mountains, the problems were enormous. These, however, were all military matters. Ominous though they were, they were still the problems of war and for such San Martín was trained.

He did not despair at the prospect of desperate or bloody battles, or even at the prospect of possible defeat.

Worry over other matters, however, wore away his strength. His health began seriously to fail. He lost weight and was unable to sleep. The chronic ailment of gastric ulcers was very nearly out of control. Several bad hemorrhages almost cost him his life, and in the face of the constant pain he was able to keep going through the use of heavy dosages of the only pain-killer available—raw opium.

Chapter 6

OTHER PROBLEMS BEGAN TO PLAGUE San Martín. They were almost all of a political nature. He believed it absolutely essential for Argentina to establish a strong, central type of government. It should be a democracy—of this he was convinced—but at the same time he felt it should have enough strength and built-in stability to withstand the destructive forces which the politically unprepared citizenry would be sure to bring against it. A weaker system, even though perhaps more democratic, which relied on the ability of the people to compromise, to give and take, would have no chance.

For example, when the question was being debated as to what *type* of democracy Argentina would have, there was much talk of a loosely organized federal system, with the various provinces more or less autonomous and with considerable powers of their own, somewhat after the system of the United States of North America. He wrote to Buenos Aires, "I die every time I hear people talk of a federation. . . . Can it be? If an established government and a cultured nation, well peopled by artists, farmers and traders (I speak of the North Americans) have found difficulties during the last war with the English [the War of 1812] because of a federation, what can happen here? You will see that this will become a den of fighting lions and that the only one to profit thereby will be the enemy."

San Martín not only knew his own people, but knew history as well. It was precisely because of the divisiveness and the lack of certain powers of the federal government that caused the United States so much trouble during the War of 1812.

Such sentiments did San Martín little good. In spite of the influence of the Lautaro Society and of other powerful friends which he had in Buenos Aires, he quickly became the target of every slur and vile piece of slander imaginable. He was again accused of being a royalist in the pay of Spain, of being a monarchist with designs to place himself on a throne and of plotting against the rights of the common people. The attacks went so far as to malign him personally—he was a drunkard, a glutton and so on.

At first his only reply to such calumnies was serene indifference. Quoting Epictetus, he said, "If the evil that is spoken of thee be true, remedy it; if it is false, laugh at it." This seemed only to increase the venom of those who slandered him. Finally, stung to anger and then despair, he cried out in letters, "Accursed be my star."

Quite aside from the personal hurt caused by such invective, the loss of faith and continual attacks seriously impeded the effort which he was making to build the army, and would weaken it terribly in the struggle ahead. Argentina *must* start her national life unified and strong; there simply had to be cohesion and purpose among the people, expressed in a powerful government, if the hard years of war which were coming were not to be disastrous.

San Martín's expedition into Chile was not even yet recognized as a national venture. The army was not even considered an official army. In spite of the efforts of the people of Mendoza, nowhere near enough of the materiel which would be required could be produced in makeshift factories in a rural farming area. He would soon be many thousands of miles from home, leading an army against an implacable enemy. Supplies would be needed continually—most of all, munitions and money—in ever growing quantities. Only through the backing of a strong government would they be available. The war which San Martín knew would have to be fought would be demanding; it would be no hit-and-run guerrilla operation.

His continual pleas and exhortations at last brought partial results. A working government was finally established, although it was not as tightly and strongly organized as he would have wished. Juan de Pueyrredon was elected Director of the United Provinces of La Plata. Pueyrredon was San Martín's friend, but even more important than this, the two agreed completely as to the necessity of the war. Many people were hostile to these plans and did all they could to frustrate them. There were reasons for this attitude. Argentina continued to suffer reverses in the north, and many believed that if an army were to be raised at all, it should be sent there rather than sent off across the Andes to Chile. They looked upon this project as foolish, the dream of a man who was insane or, at best, the victim of grandiose dreams. A large part of the population was sick to death with war and with killing and wanted nothing so much as to get on peacefully with their own affairs. They were unable to understand that this long and costly war which San Martín insisted upon was necessary if their freedom was ever to be anything other than fine-sounding words and phrases on a piece of paper.

Luckily for San Martín and for Argentina, Pueyrredon paid no attention to such sentiments. He assembled around him a group of men—such as Tomas Guido, San Martín's old friend General Belgrano and others—who had complete faith in the project. In July of 1816, San Martín and Pueyrredon met in a famous conference in the town of Córdoba. For two days they discussed every aspect of the situation, and Pueyrredon promised that the Army of the Andes from this point on would have the entire official backing of the government and that supplies would be forthcoming to help equip and maintain it. After this interview, San Martín returned to Mendoza comforted by hope for the future. His heart was lighter than it had been in two years of bitter anxiety.

One of Pueyrredon's first efforts was to sell San Martín's project to the people, to make them understand the need and to arouse popular support for it. In this effort he was backed wholeheartedly by the immensely powerful Lautaro Society. The attempt to educate the people was successful, and sentiment began to grow in the country that the Army of the Andes should be backed.

In spite of this, Pueyrredon's task was not an easy one. The government was new, still beset by internal dissension and not easily controlled. Beyond this, it was plagued by other wars on all sides which had to be fought.

The Portuguese in Brazil were again invading down through Uruguay and were biting off whatever choice pieces of territory they could get away with. In the north, the Spaniards continued to threaten. And, worst of all, throughout the entire country, small local insurrections of diehard dissidents had to be dealt with. There were no arms or ammunition for all these armies. Many of the troops went into action half naked, doing their fighting with bare swords and lances. All these things kept the hard-pressed government in a state of near-bankruptcy. There simply was not enough money to go around.

Nevertheless, Pueyrredon was true to his word and somehow managed to send San Martín much of the material he requested. By November of 1816, the last of the most urgently needed supplies had been sent by *carreta* on the long trip to Mendoza. San Martín would soon be leaving and, in any case, Pueyrredon had scraped the bottom of the barrel. The country had been drained of equipment; the national treasury was empty.

A letter which he wrote to San Martín and sent along with the last contributions reflected much affection and good humor and, also, the total exhaustion of the nation. Pueyrredon wrote, in part,

Besides the 4,000 blankets sent from Córdoba, there go now 500 ponchos, the only ones I have been able to find. Here go the 1,000 arrobas [1 arroba = 25 pounds] of jerked beef which you request by the middle of December. Here go the clothes you ordered. If there should be a shortage of blankets, have recourse to asking for donations. It is better to beg when there is no other choice. Here go forty saddle blankets. By separate post go the only two bugles I have been able to find. In January there shall be sent you 35,000 pounds more of jerked beef. Here go the 2,000 sabers you request. Here go 200 tents and there are no more. Here goes the World. Here goes the Devil. Here goes the flesh. I don't know how we shall ever extricate ourselves from the debts I have incurred. One of these days I shall just go bankrupt, thus canceling everybody's bills, and join you, so you can feed me the jerked beef I have been sending you. Hell!!! Don't ask me for anything else if you don't want to hear I have been found hanging from a rafter in the fort.

They say in South America that "until you have seen the Andes, you have never seen mountains." True or not, it is certainly a fact that even a glimpse of the foothills of these fantastic peaks is something never to be forgotten.

The Andes are a part of a great chain of mountains which stretches from Alaska to Cape Horn. In Canada and in our own country, the Rockies are a part of that chain. It extends on down through Mexico and Central America, and in Panama it flattens out briefly to a mere swelling in the earth's crust a few hundred feet high and submits to the cuts of the Panama Canal.

Beyond the isthmus, however, the mountains rear upward again and march in awesome majesty for thousands of miles to the tip of the continent. In jagged range after range, the colossal granite escarpments and glaciers roll southward. Here are to be found the greatest concentrations of sky-piercing peaks in the whole world. Nineteen, twenty thousand feet high and more, dozens of stupendous battlements rear upward and hurl a grim challenge to anyone foolhardy enough to brave them. The mountains of North America, even Mount McKinley, are mere pinpricks beside them.

There were five of these great ranges or spurs between San Martín and his destination in Chile, and one of San Martín's most serious problems was that of the choice of a route across. At that time there were passes through the mountains, just as there are today. For centuries, back to the times of the Incas, these had been known to explorers and to adventurous merchants. In 1817, there were five known routes along a 1,500-mile front. These passes were all precipitous and dangerous in the extreme, usable for large numbers of men loaded with equipment only in the summertime, which in that part of the world comes during the first part of the year.

For three years San Martín had studied each of these five routes in minute detail. Shepherds and traders continually brought information to him on the latest conditions—the state of the trails, news of disastrous slides and so on. Spies, engineers and surveying parties combed each pass from one end to the other, making maps and supplying vital information about possible sites for relief huts, places where firewood could be stacked and forage for the animals stored, slopes where passable trails could be cut in the stone and ice, likely locations to anchor suspension bridges and the like. San Martín himself had even ridden over some of the passes in order to see with his own eyes what would have to be faced and to prepare for it.

Two main routes were finally selected for the passage of the bulk of the army and its supplies. Smaller detachments would go by other routes. The two main passes were Los Patos and the famed Upsallata, where today a colossal statue, the "Christ of the Andes," stands on the border between Argentina and Chile. Each of these passes wound a tortured way between towering peaks, and nowhere on either of them did the elevation fall below 9,000 feet. Most of the distance was more than 12,000 feet above sea level.

The actual routes chosen had to be a well-kept secret until the very last moment. Men and animals would have enough trouble simply making the trip without having to fight the Spanish on the way across. Truthfully, to have made the crossing in the face of enemy opposition would have been impossible. San Martín wrote, "Each of these routes has such narrow passages that fifty men, in a defective fortification, are enough to defend them." The thought of having to do battle to get past such places must have given San Martín nightmares. He confided his choices to no one until the actual moment of leaving Mendoza.

This need for secrecy had another aspect also. The total number of troops the Spanish could muster was considerably greater than the total number of men in the patriot army. It was essential that somehow the enemy be made to divide his forces. San Martín accomplished this by writing fake documents and letters and by spreading false rumors as to the date of departure from Mendoza, and the routes the army would use. It was accomplished by the very efficient system of spies and "fifth columnists" which had been organized and whose members saw to it that the false information fell into the hands of the Spanish generals. The system worked to perfection. The

Spanish wound up in such a state of confusion that their only solution was to divide their troops and guard the exits of all of the five possible routes.

At last all was in readiness. For better or for worse, by the end of 1816, the Army of the Andes was as prepared as it would ever be. There was little more that could be done. Sweat and toil, scheming and conniving had equipped the army to the point where it was probably the most effective group of fighting men the New World had seen up to this time.

The force was composed of about 5,200 men and officers, divided into infantrymen, mounted grenadiers, artillerymen and engineers. In addition to these, there were large numbers of horsemen to help with the transport, the British medical unit, commissary people and so on.

Years of training had taught each officer and soldier the part he would have to play in the drama ahead. The enemy was confused as to the route they would take through the mountains. A vigorous, underground propaganda war had been going on in Chile for months, with secret agents demoralizing those Chileans who might be expected to be loyal to Spain, and organizing for action those who might favor the cause of independence. Other patriot armies in Latin America might fight hundreds of useless battles, dying bravely but hopelessly. If he could help it, San Martín would have none of this. The cause of freedom had been entrusted to him; he would use every bit of his skill, knowledge and genius to see to it that those who fought with him did so effectively and with no more suffering than was necessary.

So, as the fateful year of 1816 drew to an end, all was ready, waiting only for San Martín to give the "let's be on our way" signal. The snow was melting on the flanks of the great mountains; the high passes would soon be open. The Cordillera was waiting, and beyond it, the enemy.

He set the date of departure for January 18, 1817.

Chapter 7

IN ADDITION TO HIS military abilities, San Martín also had a sure touch for the dramatic and a deep understanding of the emotions which motivate men. Properly inspired at the outset of a great adventure, men can drive themselves to heights of achievement far greater than those of the normal courses of their lives, and he knew it. Accordingly, San Martín planned a gigantic religious and patriotic fiesta for January 17, the day before the scheduled departure of the army.

Outside Mendoza, in the foothills, was a wide plain called Plumerillo. Here was the army's main encampment, with shops, barracks, corrals and stables for the animals and an enormous open area which had long been used for training purposes.

Early on the morning of the 17th, the entire army was drawn up in parade formation on the field at Plumerillo. Then, with San Martín riding at the head, it marched to Mendoza. Silently, with no sound but the steady tramp of thousands of feet, the men headed toward the church on the main plaza of the city. They were greeted quietly by a vast multitude of people—old men, women, children, farmers, shepherds and others who would not be going to the war. The streets of Mendoza were strewn with flowers, and the buildings along the route of the march were decorated with flowers, brilliantly colored tapestries and banners.

The soldiers assembled in the big plaza in front of the church, where a stand had been erected. San Martín ascended the stand. In his hand he carried a long staff. Baring his head, he unrolled the staff and unfurled a beautiful flag. Declaring that the good Virgin herself had been proclaimed patroness of the army, he lifted the flag that he proposed to carry to Lima. He had designed it, and it had been stitched and embroidered by Remedios and other ladies of the town. It consisted of a broad horizontal azure stripe and a broad white stripe. On its field were a laurel and olive branch and above them two hands lifting the red liberty cap to mountain peaks and a rising sun. This flag was carried through all the years of war which lay ahead and today is a treasured memento of the Army of the Andes, guarded in the cathedral at Buenos Aires.

The vast throng of soldiers and civilians was quiet as the lovely banner waved overhead, against the backdrop of the church and the shining white mountains beyond. San Martín broke the deep silence; his powerful voice cried out, offering the flag as a symbol and calling to the soldiers for their oath of allegiance.

"Soldiers," he said, "this is the first independent flag to be blessed in the Americas."

Now the people went wild with shouts of acclamation, with *vivas* and cries of "long live our country."

Again came San Martín's voice, "Soldiers: swear to die in the defense of this flag, even as I swear it!"

"We swear it!" The answer came roaring back from thousands of voices, rough and harsh with emotion.

In the afternoon there was a huge fiesta and a bullfight, and in the evening much dancing.

Next morning the mules and horses were brought into Plumerillo from their pastures; saddles and packs were put in place. Oxcarts were loaded and the teams hitched. Troops and arms were ready. People streamed from the city to the encampment for last words and good-byes with loved ones. Remedios came with little Mercedes, who was then only six months old. Tenderly San Martín kissed and embraced them. Then he gave the signal: the time to go had finally come. Sadly Remedios watched them leave. She and the little baby were to leave immediately for Buenos Aires, and it would be a long time before she saw her husband again. Instinctively Remedios knew it, and her mind was filled with foreboding.

Slowly the enormous train of men, animals and equipment moved out. The army had been divided into six detachments—two main groups and four very small ones which numbered only a few hundred men each. To confound the enemy, each group was to make the crossing through a different pass. The two main units were to go through Los Patos and Upsallata with most of the heavy weapons, the others through passes to the north and south. If all went well, the various units were to rendezvous three weeks later, on February 8, on the plains above Chacabuco, a fertile valley in the uplands of Chile.

The crossing of these gigantic mountains by San Martín and his Army of the Andes is an epic tale in the long story of human courage and endurance. Even today, with modern equipment and communciations, a march across the Andes is a formidable undertaking. In San Martín's time it was infinitely more difficult. Little wonder that in Mendoza, as for month after month he had pondered and gazed upward at the ragged sawtooths rising skyward, he had been moved to write: "What disturbs my slumber is not the strength of the enemy, but rather how to pass through these immense mountains."

Aside from the supplies needed for its own survival, this army had to be ready to fight the moment it emerged from the mountains. It had to carry with it every single item for war. The quantities and the weights were staggering. Included were 9,000 rounds of ammunition for carbines and muskets, 2,000 rounds of cannon shot, 2,000 rounds of shrapnel and 600 shells.

The heavy artillery consisted of two six-inch howitzers and ten four-inch field pieces. The ponderous barrels of these guns were removed from their carriages for the crossing and placed on barrowlike conveyances invented by San Martín and Father Luis and pulled by men and mules. Most of the way, however, even these barrows could not be used and the guns were transported on sleds, or by hand, with special slings and blocks and tackles to hoist them up and down the sheer faces of the enormous cliffs.

Transportation for equipment, men, food and other supplies was provided by 10,600 pack and saddle mules and 1,600 horses. These poor animals perished during the crossing in numbers that are hard to believe. San Martín himself was later to write: "In spite of the most scrupulous care, more than 6,000 of the mules and 1,100 of the horses died from the heavy work, from accidents, from the terrible cold, and those that did arrive finally in Chile were in very bad condition." Before these animals finally dropped however, most of the worst and most dangerous work had been done and the men were able to finish the task themselves with the help of the animals which remained alive. Not a gun, not a cannon barrel, not a chest of ammunition was lost.

In addition to the pack and riding animals, San Martín's army, like all Latin-American patriot armies, took with it its "walking commissary"—livestock to slaughter and eat along the way. When the Army of the Andes embarked on its historic journey, over 700 head of cattle went with it. They were all consumed during the trip.

San Martín and his staff, riding sure-footed mountain mules, went through Los Patos. They moved through terrain as barren and desolate as a landscape on the moon, past stupendous mountain after mountain, "through rivers of broken rocks and volcanic ash," over icy glaciers and across unearthly chasms. Often shelter from violent hailstorms and blizzards had to be found. During these chunks of ice as big as walnuts thrummed through the air and without protection a man's face could be cut to ribbons in moments. During the days in the bleak valleys, the reflecting sun on ice and snow and granite could raise the temperature to more than a hundred degrees; a few hours later, after sunset, it could drop as low as seventeen below zero. The air was thin and without oxygen, and there was no familiar life in this strange world. Occasional stunted cacti or tufts of straggly grass grew beside the trails and on the slopes. There were no animals; nor were there any birds, except for the huge Andean condors, black specks in the sky tirelessly circling over the peaks, the snow and the ice crags and the long lines of toiling men. And always towering above, dominating the horizon for miles and miles, like a brooding talisman, towered the shining white cone of Mount Aconcagua.

Little wonder that, in later speaking of this crossing, San Martín wrote: "The difficulties that had to be overcome in the crossing of the mountains can only be imagined by those who have actually gone through it. . . . The greater part of the army suffered from lack of oxygen, of which many soldiers died, besides others who succumbed to the intense cold. . . . Everyone was convinced that the obstacles which had been overcome did not leave the slightest hope for a retreat should it become necessary; but on the other hand, there reigned a great confidence in the ranks. . . ."

The division under the command of General Las Heras was in the last stages of the trip through Upsallata Pass. Suddenly, around a bend in a deep gorge, they were surprised by a strong detachment of royalist soldiers. There was no battle; the Spanish were scouting only, as they had been doing for months. They hastily retreated, but not before they realized that Las Heras' forces were obviously powerful. They were no reconnoitering column. Quickly the word was sent back to the Spanish main command. The units which had been guarding the other passes were withdrawn and began concentrating in front of Upsallata and Los Patos.

Word that they were discovered was also passed to San Martín. He had been expecting it, of course, but had hoped for a few more days. He immediately gave orders to his smaller units to move even more quickly. Soon they were encamped in the foothills on the fields above Chacabuco, waiting for San Martín and the larger groups to emerge. By February 8, he and many of his men were through the pass, their ranks constantly swelling as more and more soldiers descended onto the plain. The Spanish also were gathering strength, even more rapidly than the patriots. The enemy was growing stronger by the moment, and San Martín knew he would have to take immediate action or the whole invasion might very easily be a failure, its fighting strength chopped to pieces bit by bit. He had planned to give battle on February 14, but these few days were denied him. He determined that the fateful encounter would be on the 11th. Many of his men were not yet through the mountains. Most of his artillery was still painfully being dragged along the trails and winched with slings and blocks and tackles across the chasms. But it was now or never. He consulted his maps, listened to the reports which patriot Chilean spies brought to him and made his decision.

The battle would be fought on the plain of Chacabuco, around an old farmhouse where the Spanish general had set up his headquarters. Very quickly, the result of all the work and all the training would be put to its final test. The necessary orders were given. San Martín had decided upon a night attack to take as much advantage as possible of the element of surprise. He called his last war council on the slopes.

"And how do we feel?" he asked a young officer.

The boy said, "Perfectly well, as always, sir."

Then, with a heavy heart, for he well knew the long and bloody work which lay ahead if victory was to be theirs, San Martín answered, laconically, "Well, bear down on the tinware [meaning the swords] until the *matuchos* [a derogatory name for the Spanish] are crushed."

He was silent a moment and then said simply, "*Vámonos*—let's go."

Silently the army filed down out of the hills, silhouetted like specters against the ghostly mountains behind them, which shimmered and stretched in the moonlight far to the east.

The royalists were still seriously split and disorganized. Most of all they were surprised at finding themselves attacked at night by an army capable of giving battle after having descended from a terrible three weeks' journey across the Andes. Their initial reaction when the patriots hit their encampment was one of panic. They were not so confused or astonished, however, that they had forgotten how to fight or had lost all discipline.

The battle was a bitter and bloody encounter and at first both sides recoiled reeling. The melee, fought by veteran and determined men ended in total victory for the Army of the Andes.

San Martín had taught his men the basic rudiments of war. The purpose is to inflict one's will on the enemy.

He had preached, "If any man resists, split his head like a pumpkin." His soldiers had learned the lesson well, particularly the Negroes, the freed slaves, who cut and slashed like men possessed. The battle was a crucial one, and each side knew it. No quarter or mercy was given, nor was any expected. Among the Spanish dead were many whose heads had been completely severed from their bodies by saber cuts.

Losses among the Spanish ran to 500 dead and another 500 terribly wounded. The ferocity of the battle can be gauged from these figures because they represented nearly 50 per cent of the effective Spanish fighting force. Losses for the patriots were much lighter.

San Martín had sent a strong detachment to the rear of the Spanish forces to prevent the possibility of any retreat toward Santiago. When the battle finally was lost, many of these soldiers managed to escape into the countryside, but in doing so they left behind them a priceless gift for San Martín: all of their artillery.

Years of civil war and political dissension had turned Chile into a huge cauldron, boiling with hatreds and suspicions. The victory at Chacabuco by the Army of the Andes did little to calm the situation.

Nobody in the capital city of Santiago knew really what to expect from this "new" army which was approaching the city, even though it called itself an army of liberation. After all, in spite of what its leaders said, it was largely an army of foreigners, invaders who had come across the Andes from far-off Argentina. Those who were partisans of the revolution against Spain and had sided with O'Hig-

gins felt little fear, but large numbers of the population
had remained loyal to Spain and sided with the royalists,
and these were wild with fear now as reports and rumors
about the fate which awaited them raced through the
countryside. As the jubilant Army of the Andes approached Santiago it passed through a scene of the wildest
confusion. Reports state that the roads were clogged with
more than 50,000 refugees. Some were returning happily
to their homes in the city; others were fleeing in mortal
terror from it.

Nevertheless, a great welcome had been prepared for
the army. Miraculously, the myriad of Spanish banners
and flags which had adorned the city disappeared.
Chilean and Argentine flags streamed in the wind in their
places. At a great victory banquet, attended by San Martín and his principal officers, a lavish meal was served by
the loveliest belles of the city. Cannon salutes of victory
rocked the building and, in appreciation, the national
anthem of Argentina was sung. (Chile did not yet have
one of her own.)

This night and the days that followed were among the
happiest of San Martín's life. The time was doubtlessly
the one truly joyous moment of success and fulfillment
which he was to know in the entire long and bitter
struggle to oust the Spanish. There were ominous clouds
on the horizon, but for this brief moment the sun was
shining and all was possible.

He and O'Higgins plunged immediately into the work
at hand. San Martín was elected Supreme Director of
Chile by a grateful and hastily assembled council, but he
refused the post. His task was with the army, and there

was enough work ahead for it to keep him more than
busy. He had no time for politics even had he been so
inclined. To his delight, Bernardo O'Higgins was then
elected in his place; together they established a branch of
the Lautaro Society in Santiago to help in the formation
of the government of the brand-new nation of Chile.

No time was wasted in passing the necessary edicts and
setting up the machinery for the establishment of a func-
tioning government. Money was issued, and provisions
were made for a school system, courts and the like. Chile
was a free country, or so it seemed, well on the road to
taking care of her own affairs. January 1, 1818, was decided upon as the day when Chile's independence was to
be declared to the whole world.

As O'Higgins and other patriotic Chileans busied
themselves in the affairs of their new nation, San Martín
had his hands very full with other problems. He had not
come to Chile to dabble in government; he had come to
fight the Spanish, and he felt that this tremendous task
had barely commenced. He issued a brief but pointed
proclamation: "We should not expect anything from
what has been done; the United Armies of Chile and Argentina must proceed with their undertaking." O'Higgins fully realized the importance of getting on with the
problem of the war against the Spanish and wholeheartedly planned for Chile to contribute what she
could.

To San Martín, the "undertaking" was a purely military one. There could be no rest until Peru had been
conquered and Spanish power totally smashed. He therefore got on with the task of creating in Chile an even

larger and better-equipped army than he had built in Mendoza.

There was only one way for San Martín to gather strength: he must start from scratch and create military power out of nothing, or nearly nothing, as had been done in Mendoza. With the help of the Chileans and the reliable Father Luis Beltran, he set up a whole new facility for training and equipping soldiers in Santiago. Chileans were recruited, and instruction began. Soon a multitude of small homemade factories and arsenals were humming in the city, turning out the supplies needed to equip them.

To San Martín's great dismay, he began to see in Chile the same patterns of petty quarreling and bickering and unwillingness to compromise for the common good which plagued Argentina. There was little he could do about it, however, except to do his task as he saw it, and build another army. Nevertheless, the political confusion saddened him. It did little to bolster his belief in the ability of ordinary men to be guided by the selfless discipline and love of honor and country he considered so important to effective self-government.

Another event which took place during these days further added to his skepticism as to the wisdom of government by the masses. He had little use for the opinions or the actions of a howling mob. To him the ease with which ordinary, decent people could be inflamed was a disturbing thing. He could not forget the incident in Cádiz when he had watched helplessly as a raging mob hacked his commanding officer to bits. And now, in Chile, another similar incident took place, and it did little to increase his trust in the wisdom of "the voice of the people."

In Santiago, one of the governor's most bloodthirsty lieutenants had been a Spaniard named San Bruno. San Bruno was a sort of chief torture-master, and torture and mutilation had been his specialties.

This man was taken prisoner by the patriots and scheduled to be tried. Then, in spite of all that the authorities could do, a mob attacked the jail and seized him. He was stoned and beaten; his eyes were gouged out in a perfect fury of insane mob vengeance. Finally, more dead than alive, the blood-covered man was hanged.

San Martín was shaken to the core by this evidence of mass "justice." He was a soldier; he did not hesitate when the time came for killing, but this was something else. The insanity of mob action was beyond his comprehension. Its ever latent presence was something which disturbed him deeply.

There now also began to develop in Chile a military pattern which was to repeat itself over and over again in the years ahead and was to plague San Martín to the breaking point and very nearly was the undoing of Simón Bolívar in the north. San Martín had expected it, but there was no answer as to how it could be dealt with. The problem very simply was that the Spanish were fine soldiers and in defeat they did not surrender or throw down their weapons and abandon the struggle. They merely retreated, vanishing in the vast open countryside. Here they lived off the country easily, regrouped and awaited reinforcements. Although badly mauled in the battle of Chacabuco, the survivors joined up with others who were evacuating Santiago and marched northward to unite with fresh troops coming down from Peru.

So it was that thousands of well-armed enemy troops ranged through Chile and thousands more were on ships coming down the coast. Battles were fought almost daily. Some of them were of considerable magnitude, although neither side was strong enough to inflict a conclusive blow on the other. They bided their time, and a kind of stalemate developed. San Martín was not alarmed; at the moment there was nothing he could do about it.

San Martín was still faced with the perennial problem of where to get the money to buy the munitions which small factories, or home factories, could not produce, no matter how dedicated. Chile didn't have money in the quantities needed. There was only one other place, and shortly after he had settled down after Chacabuco, he made a decision.

San Martín rarely took time out for lunch, preferring to eat standing in the kitchen of his residence in Santiago. One "lunchtime" he looked at his aide. "O'Brien," he said, "we are leaving tomorrow for Buenos Aires."

"Yes, sir," snapped the young man. And then as the full realization of what San Martín had said hit him, he blurted out, "But . . . but the Goths? The *matuchos*?"

San Martín seldom took anyone into his full confidence on military matters, and he did not do so now. Las Heras and other reliable generals could be trusted to keep the Spanish busy and not to lose what had been gained. And in any case, the enemy was still poorly prepared and would be for some time to come until more reinforcements arrived. San Martín did not believe that there was immediate danger.

He answered the young officer's question with, "We'll wear what we have on, of course." And that was that.

Before he left Santiago for Buenos Aires, the Chileans voted him 10,000 pesos to cover the expenses of the trip. He declined the money, insisting that it be used to establish a library, and ended his refusal with the words, "Education is the master key. . . . I wish that everyone could learn the sacred rights which make up the conscience of free men." He well knew that the sword is far from enough to make a people or a nation free.

Riding his trusty mountain mule again, he started the trip back across the Andes and the pampas to Buenos Aires with a servant and a few companions.

The long and dangerous march was finally over. San Martín entered Buenos Aires incognito and went directly to the house of his in-laws, the Escaladas. His reunion with Remedios and his little daughter was joyful, but at the same time terribly sad. A new and frightening worry had been added to the burdens which he already carried. His young wife had developed tuberculosis.

Chapter 8

BUENOS AIRES WAS STILL in a state of excited celebration over the victory at Chacabuco. Chile had been freed. A hard blow had been dealt to Spanish power. Even though the road to Peru was not yet wide open, at least a springboard for the invasion of that distant land had been established. The wisdom of San Martín's continental strategy was becoming apparent even to the most skeptical, for already the pressure on Argentina's northern border was lessened as the Spanish withdrew troops there to send them to Peru and to Chile.

The presence of the victor of Chacabuco in Buenos Aires could not long be kept a secret. Shortly San Martín was the hero of the hour, the object of the wildest acclaim. This was distressing to him. He had not come to the city to bask in adulation. He found such demonstrations embarrassing and completely out of place, as in his mind the war for independence was still far from won. There was certainly cause for rejoicing, but there was still much serious business to be done.

Nevertheless, he was entertained at numerous magnificent fetes and banquets in spite of his protests. He was also showered with valuable presents, all of which he refused. He was also appointed brigadier-general in the Argentine Army, and this post, too, he refused to accept, saying, "I consider myself more than enough rewarded. . . . It is the only reward which can satisfy the heart of a man who does not aspire to anything else. . . . Long ago I gave my word that I would not accept any high rank or military position and . . . I hope you will not attribute my returning this appointment to excessive pride. . . ."

The selflessness of San Martín was beginning to puzzle people, and to disconcert those who would have presented him with a slice of the moon if they had been able to get it. They found it hard to understand his attitude, for the common rule for many of those in power was to grab everything they could in a scramble to help themselves. San Martín's refusal of magnificent gifts and high office caused his contemporaries, in no little bewilderment, to dub him the "hero of the resignations."

San Martín had come to Buenos Aires for money, for help to continue on to Peru to finish the task of destroying Spanish power. He had a vision of two strong nations —Chile and Argentina—governed in freedom and in justice from Buenos Aires and Santiago, and stretching from the Atlantic to the Pacific. Its peoples would be united in peaceful brotherhood, assisted by the Lautaro Society in the early years of the difficult task of establishing good governments.

He believed that the realization of this dream was particularly important because of the common enemy to freedom which each faced. Cooperation was imperative;

only through it could permanent peace be achieved. From a military standpoint, the Argentine Army of the Andes had to be transformed into a United Army composed of Chileans and Argentinians, and supported by each nation. In addition, each nation had to contribute to the creation of a United Navy or Fleet, to defend the coasts against the warships which Spain was already assembling in Cádiz to send against the Americas. For all these things, much goodwill was necessary as well as money. Only by working together, San Martín felt, could these enormous tasks be successfully concluded.

To this end, Chile sent ambassadors to Buenos Aires. When all the festivities and public celebrations were done, San Martín settled down to work with them, with the members of the Lautaro Society, and with representatives of the Argentine Government. In his mind unity would be easy to achieve because of the aura of goodwill which existed at the moment and because of the great benefits which would come from it. It was not all that simple. As San Martín was becoming increasingly aware, cooperation and compromise did not come easily to his people. Nevertheless, after lengthy conversations and heated discussions, the job was done. Agreement was reached on all points. The Chilean-Argentine Alliance was created, the first of its kind to be hammered out between free and independent American states. In an atmosphere of cooperation and mutual assistance, the war was to be continued on a continental scale against the Spanish.

With the future apparently brighter than it had been for a long, long time, San Martin left Buenos Aires and

headed westward toward the towering mountains and
the battlefields of Peru. But long before Peru, there were
other battles to be fought and problems to be solved.

First among these for San Martín was the matter of
his health. He was suffering agonies from arthritis and
rheumatism, but his stomach was the principal problem.
Sleeplessness, overwork, the continual motion of riding
horseback and rough army food had aggravated the ulcers
to the point where the pain was unbearable. In those days
little was known about this malady. There was only one
known remedy: something to kill the pain. In San Martín's case, this continued to be ever-increasing dosages of
opium. In order to keep going he was by now taking the
drug in such quantities that its effects were debilitating
and stupefying. He was fully aware of this and managed
to keep the use of the drug under control, but for many
years he waged a lonely and bitter battle, balancing over-
use against the miseries of the pain which it alone could
relieve.

But there were other, more immediate problems. Rumors and dispatches which reached him in Buenos Aires
and which continued to reach him on the long journey
back did not paint a rosy picture of conditions in Chile.
When he arrived, his fears were confirmed.

He found fear and confusion among the people. There
were many who were still outright royalists and in no
way welcomed the patriot armies or the efforts to establish a democratic government. They either were openly
hostile or, what was even worse, formed a dangerous
"fifth column" which worked secretly with the Spanish.

Included were many middle- and upper-class people and, strangely enough, large numbers of *Mestizos* and Indians. These latter, and their ancestors, had been under the rule of Spain for so long that it was difficult for them to comprehend any other way of life. Their habits and ways of thinking could not be changed easily.

In the face of this, O'Higgins and many others labored unceasingly to establish a working democratic government. To do so, above all, they needed peace. They could not hope to accomplish what they had set out to do if they were continually menaced by the Spanish.

Then, as now, there was no lack of "Sunday quarterbacks." They immediately began to criticize San Martín mercilessly. They said that after the battle of Chacabuco, the remnant Spanish groups could have been, and *should* have been, rounded up, defeated and thrown out of the country for once and for all. Instead, their general had gone off to Buenos Aires, leaving the job half-finished and seeking glory for himself!

San Martín's judgment had been otherwise. He had gone to Buenos Aires to take care of the most urgent matter of the Chile-Argentina Alliance. He knew well that the Army of the Andes was in no shape for more fighting at the moment. The trip across the Andes had exhausted the patriots terribly, and the battle of Chacabuco had worn them down to nothing. Weary, battle-tired, encumbered with prisoners and loaded with war booty, which had to be sorted out and put in usable shape, these men simply were in no shape for any more immediate fighting. A holding action rather than a full-scale mopping-up operation was all that could be expected of them. This had been San Martín's evaluation of the situation, and he had entrusted the handling of the problem to his very capable second-in-command, General Las Heras.

Numerous small engagements had been fought between Las Heras' men and the Spanish, each one becoming sharper and larger in scale as the Spanish skillfully regrouped and combined forces. The situation was by no means desperate, however, and San Martín continued to leave the matter to his subordinate, who finally managed to drive the enemy into the massive old colonial fortress at Talcahuano, to the south of Santiago. All patriot efforts to dislodge them were fruitless.

Meanwhile, over 3,000 fully armed Spanish troops had arrived by ship from Peru. Nothing could be done to intercept the transports, as Spain still had complete freedom of the sea and could move up and down the coasts as she wished. These veteran reinforcements brought the total royalist troops in Chile to more than 6,000 men, a very powerful force. It was commanded by General Mariano Osorio, one of the most capable officers Spain had in the New World.

San Martín now left off his work in Santiago, where he had been working night and day to rebuild and train his own forces, and took personal command of the situation.

On March 19, disaster fell.

General Mariano Osorio was not the man to stay cooped up in the protection of a fortress while he had under his command a fully armed, veteran army. He came out of Talcahuano and began advancing carefully across the countryside toward Santiago. The patriots were retreating before him, trying to trap him and to draw him away from his base at the fortress.

On the night of the 19th, San Martín despatched 1,700 cavalrymen to harass the enemy and to slow down his advance. This force somehow allowed itself to be trapped in an area called Cancha Rayada, a huge field cut and furrowed by natural drainage systems—deep gullies, arroyos and the like. Such a terrain was exceedingly difficult for cavalry, and General Osorio took full and immediate advantage of it. He ordered an attack the instant the opportunity presented itself, with all the power he had. In the confusion and the darkness, in the melee of rearing, unmanageable horses, shouts and screams, the patriot forces were nearly cut to pieces.

The "Surprise of Cancha Rayada," as this battle is called in South America, almost brought to an end the work, hopes and dreams of San Martín and the patriots who labored with him. The cause of liberty in Chile, as well as that of the rest of the continent, hung by a thread. This happened literally in a matter of a few dark night hours.

The patriot army was completely disorganized. Most of its artillery, baggage and ammunition was lost. As the remnants of the army began straggling back toward Santiago, the city went into a panic fed by the most outrageous rumors. San Martín had shot himself on the battlefield. O'Higgins had been killed. Many officers had fled by sea from Valparaiso. The Spanish were at the city gates, prepared to exact horrible punishment from the inhabitants for their treason in helping the patriots.

The government, or what was left of it, reacted in

terror. It packed up what money it had and prepared to ship it by muleback across the Andes. Wealthy citizens loaded their silverplate and their jewels in carts and also prepared to flee. Those who were sympathetic to the royalist cause rejoiced. The crimson and gold banners of Spain were taken out of closets and hung from windows to welcome the victors. One man shod his horse with silver shoes so that the victorious General Osorio would have a suitable mount for his triumphant entry into Santiago. Once more, cries of *viva el rey,* instead of *viva la patria,* echoed through the streets and across the plazas.

Within a few days, however, riders began coming into the city with other news. The disaster was bad enough, no doubt about this, but while Santiago might be in the grip of complete panic, sanity still prevailed on the battlefield. Some units of the army had been very badly mauled and suffered losses, but were retreating in order and trying to reorganize. San Martín was still alive. O'Higgins was also alive, although wounded.

The hard training and the discipline which San Martín had insisted upon paid invaluable dividends. Although the confusion of Cancha Rayada had been unimaginable, the soldiers had not lost their heads. They had retreated as hard-pressed soldiers, not as a frantic mob. San Martín's faith in the courage and the steadfastness of free men fighting for their liberty was never more justified.

As had happened before, this especially was true with one of the regiments made up of Negroes—former slaves who had been freed. This regiment was singled out by Samuel Haigh, an English traveler who was in the country at the time. Wrote Haigh, "The Spaniards have not obtained any great advantage from this blow because the Negro Regiment Number 8 stopped the first two attacking columns and because, when the Negroes finally retreated in good order, the two Royalist divisions which were trying to outflank them clashed in the darkness without recognizing each other. . . ."

Slowly the word began trickling into the city. All was not yet lost, and the cause of freedom could be saved if people would act with courage and resolution. Certain finally that the army was an effective fighting unit once again and could take care of itself, San Martín rode into Santiago. He was haggard and exhausted but filled with calm and determination. His presence infused hope and the will to carry on in the heart of the people. Samuel Haigh again wrote, "I was at the palace when the commanding general arrived. He seemed very tired and was covered with dust. He had not changed his clothes or even removed his boots in several days. However, despite his fatigue, he was in good humor."

"Do not despair," San Martín told the inhabitants of Santiago. "Do not despair. The country is still standing and it shall triumph." And further, in a proclamation, he said, "Chileans: one of those hazards that man does not know how to avoid made our army suffer a defeat. It was natural that this unexpected blow and the consequent uncertainty should make you hesitate. But it is now time to take stock of yourselves and to realize that our army is holding. . . . Your companions in arms are regathering, and the resources of patriotism are inexhaustible."

Such buoyance and optimism were catching. In no time the people of Santiago buckled down to the task of helping the dispersed army and equipping it as best they could. Jewels, silver and gold objects were turned in to the government to raise money. Food was collected, more than 4,000 mules were rounded up for transport and a huge encampment was set up on the edge of town as a rallying point where the weary soldiers could rest and be rearmed. The arsenals worked overtime turning out more equipment and ammunition.

The incredible feat of transforming a broken and defeated army into an effective fighting force was accomplished in the unbelievable time of about ten days. The patriots were granted the boon of this time because the Spanish thought they were completely dispersed and would be unable to get themselves back into fighting condition in such a short time. Osorio and his men advanced in a leisurely fashion toward what they thought was a stricken and defenseless city.

By April 3, 1818, less than two weeks after the defeat at Cancha Rayada, San Martín had his battle plans made. There was no time to be lost. The Spaniards were practically at the gates of the city, and if they were to be fought and defeated, it had to be now and, if possible, outside Santiago. He chose to wait for the advancing army on the plain of Maipú, some seven miles from Santiago. The battle, fought on April 5, was one of the most decisive in the Western Hemisphere, and on it hinged the fate of freedom in South America.

In terms of the percentages of killed and wounded,

Maipú was one of the bloodiest battles ever fought in the history of war. At the start the royalist army numbered 5,300 men and the patriots 4,900. At battle's end, and with victory in the hands of the patriots, more than 2,000 corpses and endless wounded littered the field of Maipú. European observers who witnessed the battle were appalled at the ferocity of the struggle. Each side seemed aware of the tremendous prize at stake, and the soldiers fought like madmen rather than flee or surrender. Casualties for some of the patriot regiments amounted to more than half their number. As at Cancha Rayada, some of the Negro units were particularly notable for their bravery and for the numbers of casualties they sustained.

Maipú was no overgrown guerrilla encounter. It was a classic battle of maneuver in the strictest military sense of the word, and has since been examined and "refought" in military colleges the world over. It was the sort of operation which San Martín knew backwards and forwards. He had studied this kind of troop movement in Europe for years and had taken part in a number of such "formal" battles against the armies of Napoleon.

The enemy also was European-trained, and their generals were not novices at the grim game. Included in their units were many fine, experienced officers; San Martín had campaigned with some of them years before in Spain. And here, too, were some of Spain's proudest and most battle-tested regiments. One of them was the Burgos Regiment, and San Martín had fought beside its men in earlier days. This unit's boast was that it had never lost a battle or run from an enemy throughout its long history. The battle of Maipú rewrote its tradition, but still the Burgos' brave and disciplined stand was the rock about which the royalists rallied.

In San Martín's proclamation to his men before the battle we are given an idea of the lack of equipment and the "make-do" methods which had to be taken to overcome it. He said, "Each soldier will have for this battle one hundred cartridges and ten rocks, half of which he will carry with him and half of which he will leave behind with his unit." We are made aware that he knew this battle would be fought with bloody desperation, for he added, "The wounded who cannot walk unaided shall not be saved while the battle lasts, because four men are needed for every such wounded and this would weaken our battle line."

And to his officers he had some stern advice: "I advise the chiefs of cavalry to keep behind a squad of twenty-five to thirty men to strike with their swords those soldiers who turn their backs on the enemy. . . . This battle is going to decide the fate of all the Americas, and it is preferable to die honorably on the field of honor than at the hands of our executioners."

The plan of battle which San Martín had adopted as being best suited for the terrain of the field at Maipú was known as a "parallel attack, turning into an oblique attack." It was a classic maneuver, one that required the greatest skill and courage and timing for its execution. It was little known at the time except to the most thorough students of the military sciences.

After the battle was over, San Martín wrote his report to the government at Buenos Aires, explaining what had happened and how the victory had been achieved. He showed the report to General Las Heras. Las Heras read the report, smiled and commented, "General, this that you say here—that our line was at an angle on the right of the enemy, showing an oblique formation on that flank—was, you know, the whole merit of the victory; but nobody is going to understand it the way you say it."

"That is more than enough," answered San Martín, smiling. "If I say anything else, they are going to shout that I want to compare myself to Epaminondas or Bonaparte. Down to brass tacks, Las Heras, down to brass tacks. We have destroyed the Spanish and are going to Peru. Did the oblique maneuver turn out well? Fine, even though nobody may know what it was. . . . I would rather that they do not know it, because even so there will be many who will never forgive us for having won. . . ."

San Martín was not only modest, but generous in victory as well. His orders were that the 3,000 prisoners be treated humanely, in direct contrast to the Spanish orders that all prisoners were to be killed. Others also had reason to be aware of his kindness and generosity. The entire set of documents and letter files of General Osorio was captured and turned over to San Martín. He discovered that it contained letter after letter written by prominent Chileans to Osorio after the patriot defeat at Cancha Rayada. Sure that the royalists were going to be victorious, these gentlemen had taken the opportunity to profess undying devotion to the crown and to point out that their service to the republic was only lip service and that it was given only because they had no other choice.

San Martín could not condone such actions or agree in any manner with these hypocritical individuals, but he could understand them. He was well aware of the short-comings of his fellow human beings and did not expect perfection. Accordingly, these letters were all burned and the names of the writers never divulged. Such incidents did little, however, to bolster his faith in democratic forms of government unless there existed rigid controls to keep in hand the terrible self-interest of which mankind was capable.

After Maipú, San Martín sent a lengthy communication to the Viceroy of Peru, proposing peace and suggesting that all parties get together to establish liberal constitutions and self-government for the colonies. He said, "To attempt to restrain by the bayonet the general course of opinion in Spanish America is like attempting to enslave nature."

The appeal was not answered. It fell on deaf ears. Only by bayonets would freedom from Spain ever be won.

Chapter 9

THE FIRST PART OF San Martín's sweeping continental strategy had been accomplished successfully. The battle of Maipú thoroughly defeated the Spanish. The surviving remnants could undertake no reorganization or regrouping this time. They were in full flight northward to safety. Chile was free at last of Spain and would provide a stable base from which the last campaigns against the enemy in South America could be launched. Argentina also was out of danger and could seriously get on with the task of learning how to govern herself.

Only Peru remained, but what an undertaking the invasion of this far-off land was to be! The simple matters of terrain and geography were formidable enough to dismay anyone less determined that San Martín. Overland from Santiago to Lima was about 2,000 miles across some of the most forbidding territory on earth. Jungles, mountains and deserts all lay in wait and would have to be crossed by an army on its way to Peru. And once in Peru, such an army would be exhausted and far from its bases of supply. Nevertheless, it would have to be ready to fight the more than 20,000 Spanish soldiers who were stationed there.

The recent bloody fighting in Chile had drained the patriots' war chest. The army had lost many of its best men and officers—both Chilean and Argentinian. For the invasion of Peru, more money was needed as well as more soldiers. San Martín set resolutely to work but, as always, the process of creating, training and equipping an army under such circumstances was painful. Nearly two and a half years were to go by before all was ready.

The various groups in Chile were frequently in treacherous and disruptive disagreement among themselves as they attempted to establish their government. There was little disagreement among them, however, when it came to Peru. To them the threat of reconquest by the Spanish was an eternal and menacing possibility. Although distant, Peru was their back yard and they could not forget it. It was all too clear that there could be no lasting peace until Spanish power there had been smashed.

Except for diehard royalists, the people of Chile tightened their belts. Although long since weary of war and bloodshed, and desirous of nothing so much as peace, they followed the lead of Bernardo O'Higgins and settled down to do what they could to help. In those hard-pressed and difficult days of the infancy of their republic, the Chileans worked, flocked to join the army and taxed themselves nearly to bankruptcy to raise money to pay for what had to be done.

Training camps for recruits were established and money allotted to maintain them and to pay the soldiers. Father Luis Beltran was authorized to increase his activities, and the do-it-yourself arsenals began operating at high speed. Slowly the army grew and the stockpile of munitions began to mount again.

War, however, is a greedy monster, just as much in those times as it is today. The requirements for cash were endless, and in spite of the valiant efforts of the Chileans, there were never enough funds to satisfy all the demands. The solid help of the big nation to the east, Argentina, was absolutely essential, and it was there that San Martín turned. The provisions of the alliance between Chile and Argentina had to be made to take on real meaning. They had to be more than just high-flown rhetoric on a piece of paper.

During the years which it took to build the army for the invasion of Peru, San Martín made numerous trips over the mountains and across the pampas between Buenos Aires and Santiago in search of this financial help. It was a most frustrating and time-wasting business.

The people of Buenos Aires—actually of Argentina as a whole—had by no means been able to resolve their differences and were continually in the throes of dissension. Freedom had been won, or at least partially so, but the old diseases of disunity were still flourishing. The official machinery in Buenos Aires had at best a shaky authority over the country and was always, it seemed, on the verge of collapse. The government had to contend with financial difficulties, with attacks from this dissident group or that, with steady Portuguese invasion from Brazil or with one of a dozen other threats.

Beyond such very real difficulties as these, there was also a human reaction to San Martín's ceaseless demands for more money. The security of Argentina from outside invasion by Spanish troops had increased enormously. Many people, in all honesty, could not see why they should be asked to support the proposed terribly expensive and dangerous expedition to Peru. They considered it a foreign war, an unnecessary adventure. It was easy to forget that their new freedom from the threat of the Spanish was entirely due to San Martín's "foreign adventures." They could not see that unless the war was carried to a final and successful conclusion, their own independence would be in continual danger. They could only see that the war ahead didn't seem to have much to do with them, that it would be long and bloody and fantastically costly. San Martín's sweeping concepts were too broad and bold to be easily understood. Lesser men simply could not grasp them.

The man who pushed so hard for this continued extension of the war once again became the target of personal attacks. Once more his enemies secretly proclaimed him to be a "Spaniard" who was hypocritical in his professed love for America. To others he was a glutton, a despicable martinet or a depraved drug addict. Many were jealous of his success and his power and totally misunderstood his complete lack of self-interest. They considered him a threat to themselves and their plans; he was a man who was disinterested only for the moment and actually harbored vast, secret ambitions.

San Martín was still the popular hero of the hour, but certain of his attitudes began to alienate even his admirers. More than ever he refused the gifts and honors which they tried to shower upon him. He took no joy in the celebrations which were planned in Buenos Aires. He felt that booming cannon salutes, decorated archways, poetical eulogies, flower-strewn streets and glittering receptions were more appropriate for the triumphant return home of a Roman warrior-emperor than for a very weary soldier whose work was only half-finished. Such idolatrous outbursts seemed wasteful and childish reactions from a people whose independence was still in danger. He detested the displays and accolades and looked upon them as concessions to vanity which had no place in the course of a struggle with tyranny. Such an attitude was, of course, misinterpreted. To the other calumnies was then added a new one. He was called a cold-blooded snob, a man who was heartless and who was indifferent to honest expressions of gratitude by the masses of the people.

San Martín absorbed as much of the invective as he could and put up with as much of the entertainment as was absolutely necessary, but he continued grimly with his main purpose: to raise money. He had friends, and they were good and powerful ones. They trusted him and understood his motives. They agreed with him fully about the necessity of the "Peruvian adventure," and labored unceasingly to help. Even so, their task was a most difficult one, in view of the many other problems with which they had to cope.

San Martín had his hopes on an initial budgeting from Buenos Aires of the sum of 500,000 pesos. Men such as General Manuel Belgrano, Director Pueyrredon and others, including influential members of the Lautaro Society, were finally able to get a commitment from the government for this amount of money. On June 16, 1818, San Martín left Buenos Aires and headed westward toward Chile. Instead of going directly over the mountains, he decided to remain a bit on the beloved farm in Mendoza. The passes were still choked with ice and snow. He desperately needed to give his precarious health a chance to mend. Also, he may have had premonitions of trouble over the money commitment and felt that Mendoza was a strategically located spot from where he could exert influence if necessary on the politicians of both Chile and Argentina.

In any case, his forebodings quickly bloomed to full reality. In spite of the agreements and promises, on August 22 a courier arrived in Mendoza with a note from Director Pueyrredon. It was brief and to the point. It expressed confidence in San Martín and faith in the plans for the future. And it also said that, in spite of heroic efforts, the attempts to raise the 500,000 pesos had been failures. The note ended with the bleak words, "Therefore, I have decided to warn Your Excellency, before making any engagement, against making absolutely any drafts on the Treasury."

This communication hit San Martín like a clap of thunder. He saw his hopes, as well as the hopes of South America for final freedom, melting like the snows of springtime. Without help he foresaw nothing but dissolution of the army. Soon he would be without a command. The abandonment of the campaign against Peru would simply follow as a matter of course. He reacted immediately and violently. By return courier, he sent his resignation to Buenos Aires, and to Santiago.

The effects of the resignation were dramatic in both capitals. Responsible men, face to face with such a bitter possibility, finally realized that with San Martín out of the picture, the entire revolt from Spain was truly in precarious shape and might very well end in catastrophe.

Pueyrredon wrote, "I don't know why I haven't gone crazy. Let us forget now about resignations. If circumstances made yours excusable, it is not so now and I swear to you on my life that if you persist in it, I will forthwith resign myself. We must come out of this honorably, helping each other."

Other friends came to the aid of the cause. The Lautaro Society jumped once more into the battle both in Buenos Aires and in Santiago. The result was another promise to fulfill the financial commitment.

In Mendoza, San Martín breathed a bit easier as he waited for the arrival of the money, or at least for definite word that it was on the way. He waited and waited. It did not come, not even a part of it.

In later years, when he was an old man, San Martín wrote a set of maxims, or character guides, for his little daughter while she was still in school. One of them was "Speak but little but to the point." He might have added, "Then act with resolution," for this is precisely what he did during those days in Mendoza when the entire future seemed to walk the thin edge of disaster.

A shipment of some 200,000 pesos, guarded by armed riders, arrived in Mendoza on its way to Buenos Aires from Chile. The money belonged to Chilean merchants, who were sending it to Argentina for deposit in various banks there to cover business commitments.

"Muy bien. Very well," said San Martín when he learned of this plum dropping down out of the Andean passes. He used very few words, but they were to the point, and then he proceeded to act with resolution. "The roads from here on are infested with bandits. Very dangerous," he said. And then he confiscated the entire shipment of money, giving the guards in return paper drafts on the government of Argentina.

Eventually these drafts were presented for payment to Pueyrredon in Buenos Aires. He nearly collapsed and wrote to San Martín, "If another draft comes, I shall declare the government bankrupt and we shall all sink."

Nevertheless, to his credit and to the credit of the struggling government, every one of the drafts was honored. San Martín's act of relieving the money convoy of its funds was most high-handed and bordered on outright expropriation. He was desperate, however—at the end of his own resources and weary of words and unkept promises. Strangely, this desperate act and the motivation behind it had a good effect on Buenos Aires. Several hundred thousand more pesos shortly arrived in Mendoza, raised heaven only knew how by the hard-pressed Pueyrredon and the Lautaro Society. In the course of the few years to come, a great deal more funds were supplied by Argentina, and they contributed enormously to the final ousting of the Spanish from the continent.

With enough money now at least for a good start, San Martín left Mendoza for Chile. He arrived in Santiago on October 31, 1818, buoyant and confident for the future.

One aspect of San Martín's war plans was highly unusual. It involved operations which did not have to be faced by the leaders of any of the other revolutionary movements in Spanish America. They were exceedingly costly, and a great part of the money which was so laboriously raised went to support them. This was the creation and the maintenance of a navy.

Because of the great distance and the hazards of the 2,000-mile trip from Santiago to Lima, San Martín had decided to transport his entire army and all its supplies to Peru by sea. Spain had a number of very formidable warships operating in the waters along the western coast of South America, and to overcome these the patriots were obliged to purchase and man ships of their own. Fighting ships, troop transports and supply ships all had to be provided if the 1,500-mile voyage was not to turn into a disaster.

Bernardo O'Higgins entered into the project of creating a Chilean navy with great enthusiasm. It required all the enthusiasm the entire country could muster.

Chile had no shipbuilding industry, and the vessels were assembled with the greatest difficulty. Some of them were captured Spanish warships, taken in sea battles from the convoys Spain was sending to reinforce her army in Peru. Others were purchased outright, for cash, in the United States and in England. A ship-buying commission combed both these nations for serviceable warships. A few of the vessels were quite large and powerful—the flagship, for example, which was bought in London, mounted sixty-four cannons and carried a crew of more than 500 men.

By the time the vessels were all acquired, Chile boasted a very serviceable little navy of seven fighting ships, plus many troopships and supply ships, all in excellent condition. After the world's great seafaring powers, such as England and France, Chile was one of the strongest maritime nations on earth. Certainly she was the foremost sea power in the Pacific at the time.

Chile's extremely long coastline had for centuries oriented her people toward the sea in much of what they did and thought. The country had always produced fine sailors, and by the time the warfleet was ready, there were a number of extremely capable men available to command it. They had had experience in battle in the course of numerous engagements with the Spanish, and were in every way eligible for the post of admiral of the new navy. There were also several capable and experienced Argentine sailors available.

In spite of this, the decision was made to turn the flotilla over to an Englishman—Lord Cochrane, Earl of Dundonald. Cochrane was a highly skilled, professional British Navy man. There are those who contend he was one of the greatest fighting sailors England had ever produced, ranking with such greats as Lord Nelson. However, there were other aspects to his nature. He had been elected at one time to the British Parliament but was expelled from Parliament and cashiered from the British Navy because of a highly suspect stock exchange deal.

Cochrane lost no time in accepting the offer of San Martín's agents. He became a sailor of fortune in the New World, full of enthusiasm to fight for freedom and, hopefully, to carve out for himself a glorious, secure and golden life.

Just about all the epithets possible have been applied

to Cochrane during the time of his service in the Chilean Navy. One that stuck is said to have been given him by San Martín himself, and was known from one end of Chile to the other. It was "his metallic lordship," and it came from the great love which he had for gold and silver. Many of the other epithets were equally well deserved, because Cochrane was a vain and pompous man, icy in temperament and brutal with his men. Obstreperous seamen under his command were on intimate terms with the cat-o'-nine tails.

In spite of his defects, Cochrane had one powerful and redeeming feature. He was tops in his profession; he knew his business backwards and forwards. The British Navy was a hard school, and it had trained him well. Vain and pompous though he may have been, his credo nevertheless was that the place for a commanding officer during a naval battle, or in storming a coastal fort in the face of cannon and small-arms fire, was not to the rear. Cochrane led his men whatever the odds. He had his faults, but he was the man the patriots needed—skillful at his job, fearless, completely at home in the thick of battle.

People apparently went adventuring on the high seas in great style in those times. Everywhere Admiral Cochrane went, his wife accompanied him. Lady Cochrane was young, dashing, an excellent horsewoman and very much the English blonde beauty. She loved dancing, and Cochrane and his charming wife quickly became great favorites in Santiago. As the months of preparation for the invasion dragged by, they were very much in demand by Chilean society. Stories are told that on a number of occasions only Lady Cochrane's influence with high-placed Chileans saved her hard-drinking and hard-living sea dog of a husband from being summarily fired.

At first all went well with San Martín and his new admiral. Plans were made and executed in a spirit of great congeniality. It was inevitable, however, that sooner or later two men of such different temperaments would clash. Cochrane was a leader of men, not a follower, and in spite of everything that San Martín could do, he persisted in obeying his instructions as he saw fit, whether it pleased anyone else or not.

Of all the miseries that plagued San Martín and O'Higgins during this extremely trying period, the antics of Cochrane were not among the least. He had a positive talent for choosing the very worst moments to make difficult demands. For example, at this moment in Chile there were a good many very valuable and beautiful estates which had been abandoned by their royalist owners, or which had been confiscated from them. Cochrane had his eye on one of these for himself. It was a veritable little paradise of a kingdom, and he practically blackmailed O'Higgins into giving it to him. There was such a furious cry of outrage from the people that Cochrane was forced to sell the estate and give the money to the government. From then on he never ceased complaining about how he had been robbed, and used it as an excuse to increase his demands in a dozen other ways.

Another time, when the frantic government was down to its last peso, and facing tremendous obligations for supplies of every kind, Cochrane insisted upon instant payment of the overdue back pay for his entire navy.

Either this, or that he personally be given not his usual 50 per cent, but a full 100 per cent of the value of all prizes he took at sea. At times these prizes were exceedingly valuable. For example, on one occasion a Spanish warship was captured, in itself a very valuable prize, which carried in its chests over 60,000 pesos in gold. Cochrane usually got most, or all, of that which he demanded, under the threat of sailing off to greener pastures, where his services would be more appreciated, presumably with half the fleet.

San Martín and O'Higgins surely had much to complain about over the activities of their "metallic lordship" admiral. He was a sore trial to them, but they needed him in the worst way. While the army to invade Peru was being trained and equipped, Cochrane kept the Spanish warships immobilized behind the big cannons of the fortress at the Peruvian port of Callao. He rampaged most effectively up and down the western coast of South America, bombarding forts, destroying naval facilities and supply dumps and harassing Spanish sea supply routes. In general, he kept the enemy very much off balance and highly occupied trying to deal with him.

San Martín and O'Higgins knew this, were grateful for it and consequently put up with a great deal.

Chapter 10

MEANWHILE, THE HARD, GRINDING WORK of building up the army continued. Difficulties for San Martín and O'Higgins seemed to snowball.

Chile had strained her financial resources right up to the snapping point and teetered on the brink of fiscal calamity. More and more San Martín had to turn to Buenos Aires, and increasingly this became a frustrating and agonizing business. It hardly seemed possible, but day by day Argentina was sinking deeper and deeper into political chaos and shattering civil war. San Martín's friends—particularly General Belgrano and Director Pueyrredon—had been ousted and were in semi-disgrace. Even the reliable Lautaro Society was losing its power in the face of the general confusion. Nevertheless, whatever the situation in the government, and to the eternal honor of Argentina, the nation did not welsh on her commitments. Somehow, money was begged, borrowed or stolen and sent to the hungry army across the mountains.

During this time, San Martín continued to make trips to Buenos Aires, returning each time with some money, with promises of more and with an ever-deepening sense of imminent disaster. That which he wanted and needed so badly—a strong and stable Argentina united behind him—was not to be. On the contrary, the country seemed to be sliding more and more toward disintegration.

His own health also continued to deteriorate. He needed rest in the worst way, but there was no time for it. On one of his last trips across, he collapsed in Mendoza and was carried over the icy Andean trails to Chile on a litter, by relays of devoted *peones*. The rest on the stretcher apparently did him good and allowed him to gather together his waning strength because upon his arrival in Santiago he was able to talk the frantic Chilean Congress out of its last half-million pesos!

And so it went, from one crisis to the next, but through it all, the army was built. At the same time, though, this slowness gave the Spanish in Peru time to increase their own strength, which would make the ultimate task just that much more difficult. San Martín knew this, but there was no help for it. He fumed with frustration; there was nothing he could do but grit his teeth and keep at the task.

As though this were not enough, early in 1820 word arrived of a new threat which quickly turned into near calamity. Spain was preparing a huge invasion force— some 20,000 soldiers in all—to send to the New World to whip her erring colonies back into the fold for once and for all. These troops never arrived, because they revolted on the docks in Cádiz before they could ever embark. Nevertheless, the rumor of this force plunged every revolutionary government in the colonies into a black state of panic.

The Argentine government sent an urgent request to San Martín to return immediately to Buenos Aires with the Army of the Andes and other effective military forces he could find to defend the city against the prospective 20,000 invaders. Panicky politicians asked the fledgling Chilean Navy to sail around Cape Horn to do battle with Spanish warships allegedly convoying the troopships. And then came the order that nearly broke the backs of San Martín and O'Higgins.

At this moment, Argentina was in the throes of the worst civil disorders yet. San Martín's prophecy years before that it "would be like a den of lions" fighting each other seemed all too true. The provinces were battling with each other ceaselessly, and with Buenos Aires as well. Nowhere except in the capital was life safe. The only order that existed was that enforced by guns. The government was toppled by this civil strife, and the new one demanded that San Martín bring his army back across the mountains to quell the disturbances and to defend *it* against future uprisings.

Even though a thousand other matters demanded his attention, a weary San Martín pondered long and hard over this order. If he took the army to Buenos Aires, all the plans would be shattered. What was worse, if Chile were stripped of all military power, she would be completely at the mercy of the Spanish in Peru. One fact remained clear in his mind: unless the enemy was defeated in Peru, the entire cause would be lost. If the army which was so painfully coming into existence in Santiago were sent to Argentina to quell these disorders, its strength would inevitably fritter away and be dissipated in the bottomless pit of civil turmoil.

The orders from the frightened government in Buenos Aires grew more demanding, and San Martín reached his decision. The army must be used for the task for which it had been built: to fight the Spanish in Peru. The orders from Argentina would be disobeyed; he would renounce his own country. Such a stand did not come easily to him. In his mind a soldier obeyed the orders of the civilian government, always. Nevertheless, he resigned his commission and sent word that his forces would go, as planned, on to Peru and not back to Argentina.

The storm that fell on his head passed comprehension. To all the old invectives were now added new ones. He was accused of being a traitor, indifferent to the fate of his country. There was talk of a court-martial. He was held up as a common adventurer who had created an army simply to increase his own power. Worse, his personal honesty was attacked. He was said to have stolen hundreds of thousands of pesos from the Chilean treasury and salted them away for his own personal use in private European bank accounts.

Stung to the depths, San Martín did what he could to protect himself. He requested a letter from O'Higgins, detailing what had happened to the money, which, of course, had been spent on the army. And then he cried out, "It seems that revolutions open an immense field to calumny, and that the main shots are chiefly aimed at those who have the misfortune of being in command."

O'Higgins answered, outlining the expenditure of the funds and then adding, "The voices of responsible men, that of deserving patriots and that of the Government itself . . . arise immediately to vindicate Your Excellency after such gross attacks."

So it was that in his own country he was accused of treason, of thievery and of a hundred other crimes. His resignation was accepted by the Argentine government, and immediately Chile appointed him commander of all her armed forces. As a Chilean General, he continued the work.

At long last the expeditionary force was as ready as it ever would be. Chile had bled herself white in the effort to make it ready for war. O'Higgins was at his wits' end and San Martín was beside himself with worry and frustration, but there was no point in continuing the agony of preparation.

The army numbered slightly more than 4,700 men, a number far less than San Martín had hoped for, but they were thoroughly trained and well armed. They had food for many months and enough reserve munitions to last for several years if need be. One ship was loaded with cavalry horses and tons of hay and other forage for them. Into the hold of another vessel went the artillery and the shells, and in another a fair-sized printing press, for as San Martín envisaged it, this was to be a war of ideas and propaganda as well as of guns. Still another vessel carried supplies of uniforms, muskets, lead and gunpowder and everything else to equip the 15,000 Peruvian volunteers which San Martín hoped would flock to him once he had landed in their country. Rarely had an expeditionary force of the times—or of any other time, for that matter —been so carefully planned for and supplied.

Finally, the last of the men and the supplies were loaded aboard the vessels. Once again San Martín gave the *vámonos,* the "let's go" signal, to lead a military expedition into the unknown. On August 20, 1820, the sails were set and the ships stood out to sea bound for Peru.

From a headland overlooking the harbor of Valparaiso, Bernardo O'Higgins watched the ships depart. He recalled that this was the birthdate of his father, and he hoped it would be a good omen. As the fleet vanished over the horizon, he thought ironically that *he,* left behind in Chile, would need all the good fortune he could get. The burdens awaiting him were heavy. The dissension and the confusion which were growing among the population of the country would somehow have to be healed, and their causes resolved. The scars which Chile had inflicted on herself, in preparing the force which was vanishing over the sea toward Peru in the name of freedom, had to be erased.

The white sails of the fleet bellied and filled to the press of the southerly wind. Slowly the ships headed into the clear, blue waters of the great Humboldt current and set their courses toward the north.

The thousands of men in the vessels were voyaging into an unknown and dark abyss. No one knew this better than the lonely and weary man who commanded them. The voyage to the shores of Peru lasted two weeks. In those two weeks the realities of the situation into which he and his companions were venturing must have descended on San Martín with a grimness that filled his heart with foreboding. Events in the future were to prove only too well how right his intimations of trouble were.

He had prepared for this expedition as best he could, using every bit of his knowledge and skill. He knew full well, however, that no man can ever assess the future and prepare for it with complete success. What had been forgotten? What had been overlooked? What unknowns had he failed to foresee? There were no answers except the one cruel fact: once Chile had vanished into the mists astern, he was totally on his own. At a meeting of the Lautaro Society in Santiago shortly before sailing, he had been entrusted with the entire responsibility of the expedition. Whatever the final result, the burden of success or failure would rest on his shoulders. This was as he had wished it: his the responsibility and his the authority. This is the way it had to be, but the load was a heavy one.

The military situation alone was enough to give a prudent commander sleepless nights of worry. The 4,700 men San Martín had at his disposal constituted a small force compared with the more than 20,000 Spanish troops awaiting them. The Peruvians he hoped to recruit and arm were as yet only a vague hope. The people of Peru knew he was coming; for years he had flooded the country with propaganda, and his agents had busily been sowing the seeds of revolt and discontent. Time alone would tell, however, how the people of that country would react to his "liberation invasion."

In case of disaster, no help could be expected from anywhere. Argentina was so distant that it seemed a land on the far side of the moon and, in any event, he was in disgrace there, and the civil turmoil made it most unlikely that she could be relied upon for assistance. Chile likewise had her civil problems, and had already drained her resources so badly that she could not offer any help for a long, long time to come.

The odds against military success were great, but now, as in the past, they did not dismay San Martín. He was trained to cope with military problems. He had unbounded faith in the army he led and supreme confidence in his own ability to get the most from it.

What bothered him now, and had been bothering him for months, even years, was an entirely different matter. It had become almost chronic.

San Martín did not regard himself or his army as a host bent on conquest or on the acquisition of land or riches. His only purpose in going to Peru was to smash the forces of oppression and thus give the opportunity to the people to establish the kind of government they wanted. Now, however, at the end of a long, long trail, his belief in their ability to establish just and honorable systems to govern themselves had almost vanished.

Right up to the moment when the fleet sailed, he had been increasingly sickened at the insane quarreling, fighting and selfish bickering which was going on. This was happening in Argentina, but its virulence was mounting in Chile as well. He could not help asking himself the terrible questions: Is this what freedom means? Is this what "free" men do once the externally imposed disciplines of monarchal oppression are gone? Of what use was so much warfare, so much killing, bloodshed, suffering and misery if this was the result?

San Martín was appalled and repelled at the chaos created by men who knew nothing of self-discipline and who did not know the meaning of the word "compromise." Shortly before sailing for Peru, he wrote to Godoy Cruz, an old and loyal friend in Mendoza. He said, "I am going to make one more effort on behalf of

America. If this, because of continued disorders and anarchy, is not successful, I shall abandon the country, for my soul is in no mood to witness its ruin."

So what lay ahead in Peru? San Martín did not know. He believed in freedom, justice and the capacity of men to discipline and govern themselves. This belief, daily more shaky, was all he had to sustain him, and because of it, he summoned up all his courage and optimism and braced himself to make the dream come true. The task was enormous.

Of all the viceroyalties of the New World, that of Peru was perhaps the least anxious for "liberation." Although there were many highly discontented Creoles and *Mestizos* in Peru, it was as a whole staunchly royalist and the least contaminated by the idea of freedom and the sweeping principles of the enlightenment.

In 1532, an illiterate ex-swineherd named Francisco Pizarro led a ragtag band of 190 *conquistadores* against the empire of the Incas. This empire was even more opulent and more powerful than that of the Aztecs, which Cortes had overwhelmed in Mexico. Yet through a bizarre series of unlikely events, Pizarro was able to destroy the Incas and their well-organized standing army of 50,000 men and take their empire. Its legendary name was Biru; in Spanish it became Peru. Peru was the richest and most opulent jewel in the crown of Spain.

For centuries this land poured a glittering torrent of gold and silver into Spain, wealth beyond any man's wildest dreams. In return for this, Spain lavished an attention upon Peru which surpassed anything which she gave to her other colonies. Here were sent the most intelligent and gifted viceroys, the ablest generals, the finest and best-equipped troops, the most dedicated and loyal churchmen. Peru became the center of imperial power in South America. Its capital, Lima, which had been laid out and founded by Pizarro himself, became known as the City of Kings, rivaling the ancient cities of the Orient in its opulence and splendor. All trade to and from the Old World was routed through Lima, making it the most important and the richest commercial center on the continent. The city was the center of the church in South America and as such wielded enormous prestige and power. Lima's great university—the University of San Marcos—was the oldest and the most advanced in the entire Western Hemisphere. Here also was published the New World's oldest and most influential newspaper.

All these things and many others tended to make Peru the most "Spanish" of all Spain's colonies, the most loyal, the least likely to think of breaking the ties with the motherland. There was another powerful reason also for Peru's resistance to change and to the new ideas of freedom and self-government which were sweeping the other colonies. Peru was remote.

In the world of today it is difficult to think of any spot on the earth which is so distant that it is out of the reach of new ideas or lacks the means of communication to keep it more or less in touch with the rest of the world. This was not so in those times, and this was particularly true of Peru. Behind it were the nearly impassable Andes; in front of it the trackless wastes of the Pacific. For centuries Peru had dreamed away, her life relatively undisturbed by the forces that were reshaping the rest of the world.

By the time the revolutions for independence started in other Spanish colonies, Peru still lived in many ways as a colony of Spain of the sixteenth century. Her aristocrats were devoted subjects of the divine figure of the King of Spain. Poor Creoles and *Mestizos* stirred uneasily, not sure of what they wanted or how to go about getting it if they did know. The millions of Indians were obedient vassals who did what they were told.

There had been rebellions in Peru in the past, but they were put down mercilessly. In any case, they were more rebellions against immediate miseries, and were not inspired by dreams of turning the whole monarchist system upside down. There were, of course, intelligent and educated people who did stir in response to the changes that were taking place elsewhere, but their discontent and their rebellions, such as they were, were easily controlled by the army. These people were seething, however, although confused and uncertain as to what they should do. It was to them primarily that San Martín hoped to appeal.

Peru's last viceroy, José Fernando Abascal y Souza, was an able and brilliant man. His long rule, which ended in 1817, had cemented the colony even more tightly to the mother country. Revolts had been suppressed. The armed forces had been revitalized and brought to a peak of power. Successful punitive expeditions had been sent against the revolts in Argentina, Chile and Upper Peru (now Bolivia). The seaports, particularly Callao, with its enormous fortress dominating the entrance, had been strengthened. Until the devastating sea raids of San

Martín's "metallic lordship," Spanish naval ships operating from the port had had no trouble dominating the coast and keeping the supply lines open to Spain.

When Abascal y Souza was recalled home in 1817, he was succeeded by the head of the armed forces, General Joaquin de la Pezuela. Pezuela was a very able soldier and as loyal as his predecessor to the monarchy. Unfortunately, as the revolutionary movements began drawing nearer and nearer to Peru, he showed himself to be without the iron-hard will which the situation demanded. Nor did he have the long view and grasp of the tides of history which were sweeping toward him.

Even more than these things, however, Pezuela was handicapped by matters over which he had no control or understanding. Peru herself was changing, in spite of the ties which bound her to the past. A subtle but potent dose of liberalism had penetrated even her borders. The people were not as yet a part of what was going on in the rest of the world, but a great cloud seemed to have swept over the country, bringing word of the death of the past, and news of great and powerful and as yet undefined forces. The people listened, and wondered. Though they may have been incapable of believing it, they had heard somehow that the system of absolute monarchy was in its decline. Despotic government had run its course; it was in its twilight. Monarchism in Peru was an anachronism. Thus it was that Pezuela was forced to defend something that was already dying, and even in Peru the smell of its death was in the air.

Peru was, however, by and large still loyal to the monarchy, still obedient to the king. Over the long centuries though, Peruvian society had grown corrupt, lazy and ingrown. The lack of energy of the people seemed to reflect the easy tropical climate of Lima. They had been isolated too long, without the stimulus of fresh and vibrant ideas. They accepted the rewards as well as the restraints of the way of life offered by a crown which drew upon past glories and which, even in Spain, was declining. Life, for the upper classes particularly, was opulent and easy. Too many slaves and too many centuries of unquestioned power had eroded the vital hard core of spiritual strength upon which the urge for survival depends.

And so it was that serious cracks had begun to show on the rich-appearing surface of life in Peru. By the time San Martín and his forces appeared off the coasts in 1820, these cracks were wide. There were decay and indecisiveness in the ruling classes—those classes which should have been the first to unite and respond to the threat. There were also ominous stirrings from those below them.

A fairly strong Creole underground was active. Connections with the Lautaro Society had put its members in touch with other underground groups elsewhere. Knowledge of what was going on strengthened them. They incited minor revolts and mutinies in the army. There were mutterings against the autocratic and arbitrary rule of the church. All in all, there definitely was unrest in the country. Peru felt itself abandoned, on its own, for the first time since 1532. The monarchists were nervous and ill at ease. When the news arrived that King Ferdinand's punitive army had actually suffered a mutiny in Cádiz and had been unable to sail for the colonies, the dismay knew no bounds. If this could happen in Spain itself, surely the end of the world was at hand. Pezuela was forced to take Peruvian Creoles into his army, instead of the tough, loyal soldiers from Spain he had been counting on.

In spite of all these things, however, Peru was a formidable antagonist. Many people had no desire whatsoever for change and would fight it. The equipment and the leadership of the army were good even though some of the men in it were now Creoles of uncertain loyalties. It was a powerful military machine, and San Martín would be very cautious about meeting it head on.

Chapter 11

In Peru, San Martín elected to play a waiting game, rather than an all-out frontal attack on the enemy. He has been praised to the skies by some people for adopting this policy; by others he has been damned.

Even today, in retrospect, after exhaustive work done by many historians and scholars, it is difficult to pinpoint any single reason why he adopted this policy. There is one inescapable fact, however: there was probably no other choice available to him. As to why this was so, there are a number of perfectly valid causes, and the most likely conjecture is that he moved as he did because of a combination of all of them.

One had to do with the military situation. His forces were only approximately one-fourth the size of the Spanish. The chances of receiving any help from either Argentina or Chile were negligible. A disaster on the battlefield would be final and irrevocable. San Martín gave second place to none as a skilled commander, but he was also a prudent one. Little wonder that he hesitated about an all-out commitment with his army. He might have risked it, particularly when he first landed in Peru.

His army was fresh, eager to accomplish great deeds; its morale was high. The military situation no doubt was a difficult one, but by no means hopeless. San Martín must have realized this, but he hoped that by now the seeds of revolt which had been planted by his agents in Peru would have sprouted and that his presence would stimulate the people to take heart and to organize an effective rebellion. The extra arms and ammunition he had brought with him were for this purpose. He was ready to assist revolting armies in every way.

Unfortunately for Peru, and for San Martín, this did not happen—at least, not to any significant degree. Although many Peruvians did join up with him—especially slaves which he set free—there was not the general, mass uprising which alone could have increased the size of the army to a point where a confrontation with the Spanish would not have been such a long-odds undertaking. Furthermore, the old-guard, ultraconservative royalists somehow summoned up enough courage and will to fight the destruction of their way of life—not enough to deal with the invading forces effectively, but enough to hamper San Martín and to be a continual menace.

There was another reason also which locked him on a waiting course. It stemmed from San Martín's own personality. There was a nobility and a grandeur about his taking the course he did and about what he tried to do that set him centuries ahead of all those about him and raised him to a plane reserved for very few men.

Peru perhaps needed a tough, hard conqueror, one who would have destroyed the Spanish military force immediately, and then taken over with an iron fist until the people learned to grapple effectively with the problems of setting up their government. San Martín would have none of this. He insisted that he had come as a liberator and not as a conqueror. "All that I wish," he said, "is that this country should be managed by itself and itself alone. As to the manner in which it is to be governed, that belongs not at all to me. I propose simply to give the people the means of declaring themselves independent and of establishing a suitable form of government, after which I shall consider I have done enough, and leave them."

San Martín proposed to accomplish these aims in enlightened ways, and in view of his background and training this is remarkable. He was a stern disciplinarian, a product of the autocratic Spanish Army, with personal leanings toward some form of constitutional monarchy as possibly the best form of government. Yet in Peru, he wished his actions to be guided by the strength of public opinion! Nowhere is the greatness of San Martín's vision more evident than in his words, "I wish to have all men thinking with me, and do not choose to advance a step beyond the march of public opinion. Public opinion is an engine newly introduced into this country. The Spaniards, who are utterly incapable of directing it, have prohibited its use; but they shall now experience its strength and its importance."

These are nearly incredible words for a commanding general to have spoken to the people of a country he was invading—especially in the early 1800s. How noble his sentiments and yet, in the face of the turmoil which he was certain awaited him in Peru, how impractical! Few people were as dismayed and sickened as he was at the lack of political ability and the chicanery practiced by the Latin Americans the moment they became "free," and yet how magnificently and grandly he hoped!

Thus San Martín was a military man forced to play a game of cat and mouse, the outcome of which he could only hope for. He must have been dubious about final victory because it hinged on the social and political maturity of the people, which he mistrusted. San Martín's very real and great talents were in the military field; sadly enough they did not prepare him for the problems which began to arise almost from the very moment he landed in Peru. The fact that he had to play this kind of a game was disastrous. It eroded away the morale and will of his army. It almost destroyed the entire movement for liberation in Peru, and it very nearly destroyed him.

Much to the fire-eating Admiral Cochrane's disgust, San Martín decided to land in a small port some 150 miles south of Callao. The admiral would have preferred an all-out, frontal, no-nonsense attack. In any event, the army landed peacefully.

The beginning was auspicious. The local Spanish garrison prudently fled the scene, and scouting parties fanning out inland met no resistance anywhere. Hundreds of slaves from nearby *haciendas* were set free, and they promptly joined the liberating army. They were given arms and taught how to use them. Otherwise all was quiet; the army was once again loaded on the ships and was moved further north to a landing on a beach out of reach of the cannons at Callao.

Once again ashore, San Martín slowly began deploying

his army in a large circling movement which aimed at
sealing off Lima from the rest of the country. Detached
units ranged for hundreds of miles in all directions and
fought a number of very bloody battles with the enemy.
These battles were not decisive in any sense except for
one of them, in which the invaders managed to split the
Spanish Army into two sections.

San Martín continued moving very slowly toward the
city, frequently fighting sharp skirmishes with the Spanish. This was the sort of work at which he excelled. He
might have gone more rapidly, but he still preferred to
avoid the possibility of defeat at the hands of the more
powerful enemy and also to wait and give the Peruvians
the chance to rise up themselves in revolt. He was convinced more than ever that he was pursuing the right
track as his agents brought him continual news of unrest
in Lima and in the ranks of the Spanish Army.

It was true that the Spanish were beginning to have
serious problems. There was agitation for surrender to
San Martín, but it came to nothing. Royalists and conservative Creoles still had the country under tight control. Nevertheless, dissension was breaking out, even
among the monarchists. They too were unwilling to risk
everything in one head-on military clash; they seemed
unable to unite and to decide upon a course of action any
more than anyone else. They held meetings upon meetings. New plans were proposed as to how San Martín
should be dealt with and then discarded overnight. New
generals were appointed. The viceroy was deposed and
another elected in his place. Then what the Spaniards
feared most of all began to take place: discontent and

the breakdown of discipline in the army. There were scattered mutinies. Officers deserted, as well as many men in the ranks, as patriot agents kept up a continual agitation.

There was no collapse, however. Far from it. The basic loyalties to Spain were too strong. The mass uprising among civilians and in the Spanish army upon which San Martín had been counting so heavily did not take place, and he began to be faced with agonizing decisions. There seemed no alternative but to continue on his course of encircling Lima and see what would happen.

The immediate military problem was solved by the Spanish general. Pezuela had been relieved of his command and General José de la Serna appointed in his place. He had no wish to be bottled up in Lima, and if San Martín could play a cat-and-mouse game, he could do it equally well. In fact, by now he had little choice. He was as effectively cut off from outside help as San Martín and was just as determined not to risk his forces in outright confrontation. He decided to evacuate the city and to harass the invading army from the outside.

Once De la Serna was gone from Lima, the citizens, regardless of their loyalties, made the best of their situation, and prepared to welcome San Martín. Flags of independence blossomed, and a great celebration was organized. San Martín was not taken in by any of this and would not even enter the city until a council of prominent people had been elected and invited him formally to do so. Then he rode in with a few officers, received the delegation and immediately became bored with the emotional outbursts of patriotic rhetoric. He had no desire to be glorified; he had no taste for triumphant entries. He spoke to them in simple terms. He said, "This is not a war of conquest or of glory. It is a war of new and liberal principles against prejudice, bigotry and tyranny. . . . I do not want military renown; I have no ambition to be conqueror of Peru. I want solely to liberate the country from oppression."

In spite of this, when he officially "occupied" Lima on July 20, 1821, the people insisted upon a magnificent banquet for their "liberator." A worried and quiet San Martín attended. Little here seemed heartfelt or honest, or at all to his liking. His logical mind warned him clearly of troubles ahead.

His position and that of the Spanish were now exactly reversed. San Martín and his small army were shut up in the city, while powerful enemy forces roamed outside, looting, gathering supplies and becoming stronger and stronger. Daily they became more of a menace and with increasing daring even slashed away at the outskirts of Lima. Still San Martín would not give full-scale battle. His forces were too small, and he kept waiting for the effective revolt of the Peruvians themselves.

Inside the city, San Martín's men used up their supplies. Week by week, month by month, in the atmosphere of the corrupt and to them sophisticated capital, their morale deteriorated. The dilemma steadily increased as, hoping against hope, San Martín waited for the patriotic and liberal Peruvian Creoles to organize and lead an effective revolt.

At this dark moment a terrible epidemic of yellow fever swept Peru. Lima was especially hard hit. The royalists outside suffered badly but in no way were they hurt as much as San Martín's men, cooped up in the city. At one time there were as few as 1,200 men able to stand on their feet, and most of these were too sick to be effective as soldiers.

Word came that De la Serna was planning an immediate attack to capture Lima and wipe out the "liberator" for once and for all. In making preparations to meet the expected assault, San Martín took all the money in the treasury of Peru—more than half a million pesos—and for safety sent it to one of his warships at anchorage in Ancon, up the coast from Callao.

With unerring timing, his "metallic lordship," Admiral Cochrane, chose this moment to demand back pay for himself and his men. San Martín had no money and was unwilling to use Peru's for this purpose. He felt it was not up to him to disburse funds which belonged to someone else. Thereupon Cochrane simply sailed into Ancon and appropriated the gold. Then he weighed anchor and headed his flagship for blue water. Taking a few stray Spanish merchantmen as prizes, he stopped at Valparaiso in Chile to deliver a few choice calumnies against San Martín; then he and his beauteous wife vanished for parts unknown. Later it was discovered he had sailed around Cape Horn and gone to Brazil, where he became one of the founders of that nation's navy. Thus ended Lord Cochrane's services to the cause of freedom. San Martín sadly wrote to O'Higgins, "It is impossible for me to enumerate all the crimes of that noble pirate."

In Lima, San Martín's predicament increased. His army was on the mend from the yellow fever epidemic, although it had lost many, many soldiers, and the Spanish threat to attack the city had evaporated. The choices left to him for action were, nevertheless, painful. He must have considered them in full realization that his mission was failing. Nothing in Peru had basically changed since he had landed, even though he occupied the capital city. Should he evacuate, try to sail back to Chile or risk total defeat by challenging military forces far greater than his own? His decision was to stay on, to remain faithful to the purpose for which he had come.

Something, however, had to be done. If the Peruvian patriots were unable to organize and set a government in operation, then it would have to be done for them. This was of the first necessity if this stalemate was ever to be broken. The Lautaro Society in Lima instigated a movement to appoint San Martín head of the government, with the official title of "Protector of Peru." Of this he wrote to O'Higgins, "The society has compelled me peremptorily to put myself in charge of the government. I have had to make the sacrifice since I realize if it were otherwise the country would be involved in anarchy. . . ."

San Martín settled down to do what he detested—run a government. He accomplished a great deal. The Inquisition was abolished. Finances were stabilized, the country was opened to free, international trade and all slaves were emancipated. He opened libraries and schools and endeavored to set up a just legal system. During a long year of struggle, surrounded by dangers, hypocrisies and threats of all kinds, San Martín managed to give Peru a democratic and liberal foundation upon which a nation could be built.

In spite of this, he was far from content. He felt that the adulation which the people of Lima gave him and the enthusiasm with which they "embraced" democracy were not real and could change overnight. Furthermore, he didn't truly understand the art of politics. For example, when administrative matters didn't go as he thought they should, he tended to introduce harsh and repressive measures, much as a military man might control soldiers. Back of it all was his deep mistrust of too much freedom for people who were unaccustomed to it, untrained for it and unable to handle it.

Events proved his misgivings to be correct. In spite of the laws which had been established, the people simply could not get together and govern themselves effectively. Confusion began to mount, and soon it reached the all-too-familiar state of near chaos. San Martín's popularity began to wane. The calumnies mounted. Eventually he became, instead of the glorified liberator, an "invader" who had led an army to Peru for no purpose other than to gather power for himself and grind down the people. It must have been literally unbelievable to San Martín —and all this in the face of the still powerful Spanish armies loose in the country! Calamity piled upon calamity. The worst was a report, which he could never prove, that many of the officers and the men of his beloved Army of the Andes were plotting a revolt against him. The story is that they were stung by his refusal to attack the Spanish, believing that only disaster lay ahead if he persisted in his policy of waiting for the Peruvians to rebel. They may have been right, for the slide of events was ever downward.

In the face of all this, it was natural enough that San

Martín's health began to fail badly. The problems were
the old ones—rheumatism, arthritis and the stomach
ulcers. He hemorrhaged numerous times; the pain was
excruciating, and the only remedy was the old one—more
and more opium.

He had to enter into semi-retirement in a house near
Lima and turn the government over to his assistant, a
Lautaro Society man with a considerable reputation as
an able administrator. His name was Bernardo Monteagudo, and he turned out to be one of the shrewdest,
most Machiavellian men any of the Spanish-American
revolutions had yet seen. His name is forever cropping
up in the shadowy corners of Latin-American history as
one who pulled strings behind strings and who manipu-
lated men and events with sinister skill.

Monteagudo's only answer to the dissension in Lima
and to the ever-mounting number of plots which the
Spanish aristocracy made against San Martín was terror
and more terror. His prisons were always full, his torture
chambers constantly busy. In spite of San Martín's proc-
lamations that life and property were to be respected,
Monteagudo initiated a program of banishment for all
Peninsulares and confiscation of whatever wealth they
had. The banishments were carried out with Gestapo-
like ruthlessness and cruelty. When people reported this,
or complained to San Martín, he refused to listen to any
evil about Monteagudo—a reaction which was not like
him at all. The chances are that he was so ill, or so heavily
dosed with opium, that he was uncertain as to what was
taking place. Whatever the reason, there seems little
doubt that for this brief period, San Martín was not him-

self. The Chilean envoy to Peru felt this so strongly that
he wrote to O'Higgins: "Our Liberator is not the man he
was."

During these dark days in Lima, that part of San
Martín which was a soldier continued to be clear and
precise. The habits of a lifetime were strong. Political
problems and the solutions for them may have overwhelmed him, but military matters, never. He could assess
them for what they were and take the steps to do what
had to be done.

The military situation was far from his liking. Basically, the trouble was the same as it had been: he was far
too weak and the enemy too strong. Apparently, also, he
had at last come to believe that the only solution possible
for the political predicament was a military one. Quite
obviously, his dream that the Peruvians would revolt and
destroy the Spanish Army themselves was not going to
come true. The job would have to be done for them, and
unless it was done, then the entire cause would be lost.
How to do it was another matter.

As he pondered, his mind turned to the north and to
the man who might be able to help—Simón Bolívar.
Sometime before, San Martín had "lent" Bolívar 1,600
men to help with an important battle in Ecuador. This
had weakened his own army considerably, but the risk
had been justifiable. And now, perhaps, some sort of
military cooperation might solve his own dilemma.

San Martín had been writing to Bolívar for a long
time; in January of 1822 he sent another note, asking for
a meeting for the purpose of working out a joint effort
for the Peruvian campaign. His army, plus Bolívar's

army, had sufficient strength to force a peace on the Spanish.

No meeting was agreed upon until June of the same year, at which time Bolívar wrote offering the use of the forces under his command to help defeat the royalists. San Martín answered immediately. This was exactly what he wanted. The date for the meeting was set for July, and the place was Guayaquil.

Some idea of San Martín's frame of mind and of his hopes for the future are evident in his words: "God help Peru. Yet I believe that even His supreme help could not suffice to liberate that unhappy land. There is only one man who can achieve that liberation, supported by his strong army—Bolívar."

Chapter 12

LIKE JOSÉ DE SAN MARTÍN, the man who was on his way to Guayaquil for that important meeting in 1822 was a most extraordinary person.

In appearance, Simón Bolívar was almost the opposite of San Martín. He was a small man, slender and tense. His face was not particularly attractive—it was hawklike and dominated by burning, flashing eyes—and well reflected the hopes and the dreams and the insatiable hunger for glory which burned in his passionate heart. Its lines were deep, brought on by struggle and suffering. Already the disease which eventually was to take his life—tuberculosis—had started its deadly course. At the time of the meeting with San Martín, Bolívar was only thirty-nine years old, but he is said to have looked like a man of sixty.

Bolívar was the son of one of South America's most aristocratic and wealthiest families. It had been in the colonies for more than 200 years, and its blood lines were as pure and noble as any in Spain itself. Except for the automatic stigma of being Creole, the Bolívars were the equals of anyone in the mother country.

157

As a young man, Simón Bolívar had fallen under the spell of the principles of the enlightenment during travels in Europe. In spite of his background of enormous wealth and privilege, he early dedicated his life to the cause of independence for his native Venezuela. Dreamer, starry-eyed patriot, eloquent and fiery apostle of liberty, he left behind his life of ease and turned soldier, rallying men to follow him into battle.

By 1822, the year of his meeting with San Martín, Bolívar had been fighting the Spanish steadily for more than 12 years. From one end of northern South America to the other he had led the struggle—from steaming tropic jungles to frigid Andean wastes. These were years of warfare so filled with fury and killing and violence that the mind is boggled at the thought. In some of these campaigns, he was defeated so badly that he only escaped his executioners by fleeing in exile to Jamaica and Curaçao in the nearby Caribbean.

Slowly, however, as Bolívar learned the trade of the soldier, the tide turned. Finally, in a series of masterful marches and campaigns, the ragged patriot armies which he led defeated the Spanish armies throughout the entire enormous area of what are now the independent republics of Venezuela, Colombia and Ecuador.

In direct contrast to San Martín, who was first and last a military man and who became involved in politics only when he had no other choice, Bolívar was an avid student of government and a skilled politician. He never ceased to follow up his military victories by establishing governments. Because he feared fragmentation of the great viceroyalties into small, quarreling states, he favored the creation of large, continental supernations which would have enough strength to rule efficiently and justly until the masses of the people could be educated to administer their own affairs. Such a state was his creation of Gran Colombia, a gigantic state comprising all the territories which he had liberated. Although Bolívar was a colossal egotist with a boundless thirst for personal glory, he was also a passionate believer in democracy. He would never permit himself to be installed as any kind of a dictator. He wished his people to enact just laws and then submit to them, as he himself was willing to do.

As he approached this meeting with San Martín, Bolívar rode the heady heights of power and adulation. He could do no wrong, and he was obsessed with an unshakable belief that his destiny was to be that of the man who would bring independence to Peru and that this nation would promptly become a part of his huge superstate of Gran Colombia. He planned for his meeting with San Martín full of dreams for even greater personal glory, and he was certain they would be realized.

As for San Martín, the word that the meeting with Bolívar had been arranged galvanized him back to full action. His health improved; the lethargy and indecisiveness vanished. He looked forward to the encounter with great pleasure and felt sure that its outcome would be full military cooperation between his army and that of Bolívar. He felt sure that this combined force could soon solve the problem of Peru and that this last bastion of Spanish power in South America would quickly be crushed.

In all truth, however, it would have been difficult to

have found two men whose characters and personal ambitions differed more than those of José de San Martín and Simón Bolívar. San Martín was quiet, steady, austere, inclined to talk little and always to the point. Bolívar was outgoing, impulsive, flamboyant and expansive in his speech. San Martín looked forward to retirement from public or official life of any kind, and the urge for the peace and tranquility which awaited on the little farm in Mendoza was almost an obsession. On the other hand, Bolívar envisioned himself as the eternal public figure, basking in the gratitude of the people, enjoying their homage to the hilt.

Both men were absolutely determined that Peru should be liberated and cleared of the Spanish and the war concluded, but there was a vast difference in their approach. San Martín wanted Peru to be free, but his own ambitions to take part in the campaign were secondary; he didn't care who led the armies which would defeat the Spanish. On the other hand, Bolívar's soul yearned for the honor; *he* wanted to do the job.

There could have been but one ending to a meeting between two such men. Their eyes were on the same goal, but the personal parts they were to play in its realization were diametrically opposed. From the moment that San Martín's ship, the *Macedonia,* anchored in the bay and he stepped ashore to the dock of the oppressively hot, squalid little town of Guayaquil, the handwriting on the wall was clear. The differences between the personalities of the two were obvious from the start. San Martín was in the position of "second man," a sort of "johnny-come-lately."

Bolívar had already been in Guayaquil for about ten days. He had seen to this. During this period he had made all the preparations to welcome San Martín to "Bolívar territory." These preparations were lavish. The flowers and decorated triumphal arches were in place. The uniforms of the honor guards were elegant and colorful. The bands had polished and burnished their instruments so that they shone like mirrors beneath the blazing tropic sun. As San Martín stepped on the dock, the music began and the *vivas* of the massed crowds began on cue. Bolívar stepped forward and greeted San Martín with a hearty embrace and welcomed him to the soil of Gran Colombia —in itself quite a presumption, since at the moment Guayaquil was on her own soil only, not a part of any nation.

All this sort of thing was very dear to Bolívar's personality. To San Martín it was but empty flattery, the very type of hollow public acclaim which he for years had been trying to avoid. A little girl approached him on schedule and placed a crown of gold and laurel on his head. San Martín's distaste was painfully apparent. He removed the crown, saying, "I don't deserve this demonstration. There are others far more worthy of it." And then his innate courtesy caused him to add, "But I shall preserve this present because of the patriotic sentiment it expresses. This is the happiest day of my life."

After San Martín had been installed in a sumptuous dwelling on the edge of town, the two men started their meetings. No one else was present at them. No notes were kept. Neither man ever revealed exactly what was discussed or what conclusions were reached. From their subsequent actions, dropped fragments of conversations and letters, many educated guesses have been made as to what actually did happen at the confrontations. Otherwise, it has been one of history's best-kept secrets.

San Martín apparently was so disillusioned with what had happened to attempts at self-government in the lands which he had liberated from Spanish rule that he is said to have suggested the establishment of strong, constitutional monarchies until such time as the people were ready for democracy. Bolívar would have none of this. He fully realized that the governments he himself had set up in the wake of his successful military campaigns were already seething with dissension and quarreling, but he still would have no part in any kind of a monarchal arrangement. He felt it would be a gross betrayal of his romantic dreams of freedom and democracy.

The night after the first meeting a grand ball was held. Bolívar danced the night through, but after one courtesy dance with a local belle, San Martín retired. He needed the time to work up a new set of proposals which Bolívar might be willing to negotiate. What these proposals were we shall never know. During the night word came of a terrible uprising among the troops and the members of the government headed by San Martín's man, Monteagudo, back in Lima. Monteagudo was said to have barely escaped with his life and was in full flight northward to Panama. This act of rebellion crushed San Martín. He was broken in heart and in spirit, with all his bargaining power destroyed in the discussions with Bolívar. Two subsequent meetings accomplished little.

Whatever the general areas of disagreement were between these two men, on one matter they were in agreement. This was the military situation in Peru. It was terrifying, as San Martín had every reason to know. Bolívar knew this also, but tended to underestimate its seriousness. But even in this matter they could not agree on how to resolve the problem. The question of military cooperation, which in San Martín's mind was of utmost importance, found them only in disagreement.

San Martín offered to contribute his own troops to a united military command. Bolívar avoided the proposal. San Martín then offered his own troops and himself as well, to serve under the command of Bolívar until the war was won. Bolívar also refused this, and to San Martín the reasons were evasive and not at all sincere.

Eventually it became clear to San Martín that Bolívar intended to liberate Peru himself and had no intentions of sharing the glory with anyone. It then became simply a matter of the most selfless man retiring, and this is exactly what San Martín decided to do. He determined to turn his army over to Bolívar and retire absolutely from any official position from that point on.

Another great ball was planned for the last night in Guayaquil. It was ablaze with glittering uniforms, lights, music and champagne and graced with lovely ladies. San Martín had never been comfortable in such a situation, and so at a very early hour he kissed the hand of his hostess in a polite token of farewell. Then he turned to his aide and said, "Let's get out of this riot." The two of them slipped out and made for the pier and the waiting small boat to take them out to the *Macedonia*.

Bolívar saw him go and followed him. The two men

talked again privately, at great length, in the darkness of the pier. When the moment came for departure, Bolívar stepped forward to embrace the older man. San Martín held him off and was heard to say, "General, only time and events will say which of us has seen the future with more clarity."

Then San Martín climbed into the small boat and, was rowed out to the waiting vessel. The sails were loosed to catch the night breeze, and the ship headed southward to Peru. The meeting, upon which so much depended and for which San Martín had had such high hopes, was over.

The night was lit only by the blue glimmer of millions of blazing tropic stars; in the sooty darkness San Martín paced the decks. His mind must have been filled with a multitude of thoughts and impressions of the last few days. What they were no one will ever know, as San Martín was not the man to take anyone completely into his confidence. We have an inkling, however, because he turned to the companion sharing this night stroll with him, and said, *"El Libertador nos ha ganado la mano."*

But even this is enigmatic. How is it to be translated? What exactly did San Martín mean? The phrase is idiomatic and conveys many meanings, depending upon the context of the situation in which it is used—for example, "The Liberator has won the hand." Or "has won this round," or "has gotten the jump on us" or "has beaten us to the starting post." And so on.

Nobody will ever know for sure what San Martín meant, but the most accurate explanation is to be found in a letter which he was to send to Bolívar immediately upon his return to Peru. It confirmed briefly the topics which they had discussed and then went on to say: ". . . The results of our interview are not those which I foresaw for a quick end to the war. Unfortunately I am completely convinced that you have not deemed sincere my offer to serve under your orders with the forces at my command, or that my person is embarrassing to you. The reasons that you advanced . . . have not seemed very plausible to me. . . ."

Then he continued, with his usual pithy clarity, to evaluate the military situation in Peru. He issued a blunt warning to Bolívar: ". . . Do not indulge in any illusions, General. The information which you have about the Royalist forces is wrong. They number, in Upper and Lower Peru, more than 19,000 veterans, who may unite within two months. The patriot army, decimated by illness, will not be able to send to the front more than 8,500, and of these a great part are raw recruits. . . ."

Going on, he said:

. . . General, my decision has irrevocably been made. I have called the First Congress of Peru for the 20th of next month and on the day after its installation, I shall embark for Chile, satisfied that my presence is the only obstacle which prevents you from coming to Peru with the army at your command. . . . Having no doubt that after my going, the Peruvian Government will request the active cooperation of Colombia and that you will not be able to refuse such a demand, I shall send you a list of all the officers whose conduct, both military and private, may commend themselves to you. . . . For me it would have been the acme of happiness to end the war of independence under the orders of a general to whom America owes its freedom. Destiny orders

it otherwise and one must resign oneself to it. . . . With the feelings and with the hope that you may have the glory of ending the wars of Independence of South America,
I am your affectionate servant,
José de San Martín.

As a farewell present, San Martín sent Bolívar a shotgun, a pair of pistols and his own personal horse. Bolívar, on his part, sent San Martín a portrait of himself. Perhaps nothing so much illustrates the personality differences between these two very great men as their choice of gifts for each other.

The story of the independence movement in South America would not be complete without rounding out briefly the tale of Simón Bolívar and his armies in Peru subsequent to the meetings with San Martín.

As San Martín had known very well, the final expulsion of the Spanish from Peru was not a simple matter. He had seen this from the beginning. The royalists were simply too powerful to defeat quickly without the help of a massive uprising of the Peruvians. This revolt did not take place in time to help him and his United Armies of Chile and Argentina. Nor did it take place in time to help Bolívar as he started his campaigns.

By this time Peru was a lost, isolated little enclave, the last remnant of Spain's once mighty imperial power in South America. Its people felt themselves abandoned, betrayed and deserted by their mother country, which indeed they were. The loyalty to the homeland never faltered, however, nor did the fighting capability of the armed forces. The Spanish soldiers in Peru fought desperately, to the bitter end.

The defeat of this Spanish Army was a slow, grinding and, above all, appallingly bloody business. It was not over until 1824, when the final battle took place on the sky-scraping plateau of Ayacucho, deep in the Andean wilderness. San Martín's troops, Bolívar's army and thousands of fresh soldiers sent down from Gran Colombia were finally able to do the job.

Even then, the agony was not over. A large Spanish force under the command of General José Ramón Rodil, along with great numbers of still-loyal *Peninsulares,* managed to fight their way into the great fortress at Callao and were never defeated in battle. Looking all the while to the sea for the help which never came from far-off Spain, they were literally starved out. Loyal to the end, when the last rat had been eaten and all hope of assistance was gone, they sorrowfully hauled down the crimson and gold banners in surrender and crept out to take up what was left of their lives as best they could.

Mention should also be made of San Martín's beloved Army of the Andes. The last remnants of all those who had left with San Martín came home finally—not more than a hundred in all—in 1826, after having fought from the River Plate to the mountains of Ecuador, campaigns which had lasted more than twelve years and covered more than 10,000 miles. The arms of the last seven of these men who rode so wearily into Buenos Aires were presented to the government of Argentina, and today are carefully preserved as mementos of the past and of the heroes who struggled so long and so bitterly for freedom.

The years of life that remained to Simón Bolívar after the final liberation of Peru were not years of triumph and glory. Instead, they were years of disillusionment and heartbreak.

He died in 1830 at the age of 47, and the last years of his life were devoted to a doomed struggle to preserve the unity and the tranquility of the nations he had set free and created. Nothing worked; every hope he had had for a noble society of free men evaporated in quarreling and anarchy. At the end he was so weary and heartsick he could scarcely contemplate the wreckage. Nevertheless, he kept on trying to make his contemporaries behave and put love of man and love of country above their own interests. It was all in vain.

Eventually, as happened with San Martín, even he became suspect and the subject of the vilest calumny. He was called a tyrant, a dictator, a would-be emperor. At last Bolívar was declared persona non grata in Venezuela and Colombia, and was forced to seek exile abroad. On his way to exile, he was able only to get as far as Santa Marta, a little tropic port on the Caribbean at the mouth of the Magdalena River in Colombia. Penniless and dying of tuberculosis, he spent the last few months of life contemplating the ashes of his dreams.

When leaders of a military uprising in Bogotá wrote to him, imploring him to come and take part in it, he answered, "Believe me, I have never looked upon uprisings with friendly eyes and during these last days I have even repented of those we undertook against the Spanish. . . . My last wishes are for the happiness of my country. If my death can contribute anything toward the reconciliation of the parties or the unification of the nation, I shall go to my grave in peace."

More bitter are his last words. "America is ungovernable. Those who have served the revolution have plowed the sea."

Perhaps in the final months of his life, Bolívar had reason to recall his last conversation with San Martín on the dock in Guayaquil so long before and to remember the quiet wisdom of the weary and disillusioned old soldier from Argentina. Time and events had indeed demonstrated which of the two men had seen "the future with greater clarity."

Bolívar was buried in the church in Santa Marta, in borrowed pants and shirt. His own were in rags. Only after twelve years did the furies of rebellion and hatred in Venezuela cool sufficiently so that his remains could be returned with honor to their final resting place in Caracas.

Chapter 13

EVENTS MOVED VERY SWIFTLY for San Martín upon his return to Lima from Guayaquil. He had made up his mind as to what he was going to do, and he lost no time in the doing.

Peru had elected a congress, and San Martín appeared before it to present his resignation as Protector of Peru and to return to the people the symbols of authority he had been given.

The delegates could hardly believe their senses. In spite of all their efforts to persuade him to change his mind, he remained steadfast in his decision. Before he left the hall, he deposited several documents he had written which were to be read aloud after his departure. Perhaps as much or more than anything else he had ever written or said, they reflected his humility, his honesty and the tremendous clarity with which he viewed himself and the events in which he had participated. They remind one of the Farewell Address of our own first president, George Washington. Although they were addressed to the people of a far distant land, they deserve to be remembered always in the hearts of those who struggle for liberty, everywhere.

San Martín wrote to the Peruvian Congress:

. . . My promises to the peoples in whose lands I have conducted warfare have been fulfilled: to help them obtain their independence and to leave the election of their governments to their own will. The presence of a fortunate soldier, be he as selfless as it may be, is to be feared by states which are newly formed. Besides, I am bored with hearing that I am trying to enthrone myself. However, I shall always be ready to make the last sacrifice for the freedom of the country, but only as a private individual, and nothing else. So far as my public conduct is concerned, my compatriots (as generally happens) will be of divided opinions; *their sons will reach a true verdict.* Peruvians, I leave you with your national representation established. If you give it your full confidence, be sure of victory; otherwise anarchy will devour you. May heaven protect your destiny, and may your destiny give you every happiness and peace.

After taking leave of his heartbroken and faithful Army of the Andes, San Martín was gone. He took with him a few ounces of gold to cover the expenses of the trip ahead of him, the personal sword he had used so many years in such bloody fighting and one other cherished memento which had been presented to him by the Peruvian Congress—the personal battle standard, or banner, of Francisco Pizarro, carried with him at the time of the conquest of Peru in 1532. Legend has it that this banner had been hemmed and embroidered by Juana the Mad, daughter of Isabella and Charles V of Spain. It had been in Lima since the days of the conquest as a symbol of Spain's domination over South America. Now, that epoch was drawing to an end after nearly three and a half centuries, and it seemed fitting that the standard be taken away by the soldier who had done so much to bring Spanish rule to a close.

San Martín also wrote one further letter in Lima. It was to his old companion and loyal friend, Bernardo O'Higgins. On a personal level, he tried to explain his act of renunciation. He said: "You will blame me for not having finished the work I began. You are right, but I am more so. I cannot support any longer having them say that I am a tyrant, that I want to be king, emperor, anything, even the devil himself. . . . When all is said and done, my youth was sacrificed to the Spaniards, and my middle age to my own country. I believe that I have the right to dispose of my old age. This is the last letter that I shall write."

Perhaps O'Higgins, staunch patriot and battler for liberty that he was, did not sympathize with San Martín at that moment. Perhaps he did blame him for not finishing completely the task he had undertaken. This we do not know. However, even if he did disapprove, he himself was shortly to understand the decision which San Martín had made. He was caught up in a savage revolt in his own land, and he too was driven out, an exile, leaving his unfinished task behind him.

Of all great public figures in Latin America, San Martín has been perhaps the most unjustly vilified. When he left Peru for Chile, the final calumniations had already started. Creole politicians, monarchists—all with an ax of their own to grind—started heaping the invective on his head. He had come to Peru as a tyrant, they said, bent on becoming a dictator, or on establishing a royal line with himself, King José de San Martín, as its founder. He had ground down the people, he had robbed the nation blind, he had departed from the country weighted down with loot extorted from the nation.

When San Martín departed from Chile on the expedition to Peru, he had been at the head of a powerful army and was filled with hope for the future. Now he was returning, alone, nearly penniless, vomiting blood and crippled with rheumatism. He came back, in a sense, a failure; few people knew why he had returned, or even that he was there. And if they had known, they couldn't have cared. O'Higgins welcomed him at the port with a gun salute, but this was about all. Even this gesture saddened San Martín because the signs were all too evident that his old friend was also headed for disgrace. The government which O'Higgins had worked so hard and so selflessly to establish was by now completely undermined by the "forces of liberty." The smell of its death was in the air. San Martín knew these signs only too well; the processes of vilification and slander were working overtime against O'Higgins as the "patriots" worked ceaselessly for his downfall.

San Martín spent two months in Santiago, desperately ill, but at last he felt well enough to face the long trip over the Andes to Mendoza and reunion with Remedios and their little daughter. He had been living on the charity of a friend in a small house on the outskirts of Santiago and was joyous finally to be mounted on a good mountain mule, heading for the high passes. He was alone except for a handful of companions and a servant.

The gaunt soaring peaks and sky-piercing glaciers, so well remembered from other days, must have seemed as bleak and cheerless as his own soul.

San Martín was only forty-four years of age at this time, but he seemed far older. His once powerful physique was emaciated. Weariness and fatigue were apparent in his every motion as he slumped in his saddle. The only features reminiscent of other days were his magnificent dark eyes. They had seen a great deal; sorrow and suffering were burned in them. Halfway through the passes he was met by one of his former officers, Captain Manuel de Olazábal, who now lived in Mendoza. De Olazábal had been a cadet in one of the original grenadier squadrons of 1813 in Buenos Aires and had come to meet his former commanding officer. They met in a high, snowy pass; De Olazábal dismounted and ran to greet San Martín. The emotional shock was too great. San Martín could do nothing more than to embrace the younger man and to place his hand on his head, murmuring, "My son, my son."

The party continued on through the mountains. We are indebted for a description to Ricardo Rojas, author of the definitive work *San Martín, Knight of the Andes.* "San Martín was coming through La Cumbre, riding a fat mule, with a Hungarian-type saddle, the stirrups lined with cloth against the cold. He was dressed in a short blue pea jacket and trousers, yellow leggins and gloves; a Chilean type poncho covered his body and on his head he had a large hat of Guayaquil straw. In his sad face 'shone those eyes that nobody could describe.' "

In Mendoza, under the mild climate and with the kind

treatment of old friends, San Martín's health improved. When word reached him that O'Higgins had been overthrown in Chile, he wrote joyfully to his old friend, now in disgrace like himself, "Millions upon millions of congratulations for your separation from the Government. . . . Now you will enjoy peace, without the necessity of creating ingrates every day. . . . Enjoy the peace that the memory of having worked for the welfare of the country will give you." And then, mentioning his own penniless condition, he added, "It is indeed singular, this thing which is happening to me; doubtless it will happen to you some day, my friend. They are convinced that we have robbed them hand over fist. Ah! If they only knew. If they only knew the truth."

In Mendoza, San Martín changed his plans. He decided to move to the beloved farm and send to Buenos Aires for Remedios and their little daughter. There he hoped to fend off the woes of the outside world and pass his last days puttering in the garden and the orchard.

It was not to be. Word reached him that Remedios had taken a turn for the worse and had died. It had been four years since San Martín had seen her and now, more heartbroken than ever, he tried to decide what to do. Daily it was becoming more and more difficult. Word that came to him from Chile, and especially from Peru, was not good. In an about-face, his caluminators were now imploring him to come back and save them and the nation from total chaos!

Travelers wrote to him, "Peru suffered less in 350 years of Spanish rule than she has in one year of independence."

And another wrote, "What clamor there is in this city [Lima] about the absence of Your Excellency. The majority want you and await you anxiously. . . . There is absolutely no money. . . . The present state of affairs is diabolical."

Finally, one letter that could not be ignored came from Riva Aguero. Aguero was the politician who had led the public campaigns and denunciations of San Martín during the last months in Lima. He begged San Martín to return, with an army, to restore peace!

Stung to anger, San Martín answered that he would never stain his sword in a civil war, telling Aguero in no uncertain terms what he thought of him. Later, when he had calmed down, and had received another letter from other prominent Peruvians, he answered, "You know intimately my feelings for Peru, for America, for its independence and its happiness, for which I would sacrifice a thousand lives . . . but . . . Peru is lost, yes hopelessly lost, and perhaps the cause of America in general. You have the power of saving it; it is in your hands. . . ." And then, like the dying Bolívar, he pleaded for unity and for respect for law. "You can be the redeemers of America, or its executioners. There is no doubt. You will decide which. Take care of the complaints you may have, respect the authority of the congress, good or bad, or whatever it is, because the country has elected it, whatever it is . . . and unite as necessary. . . ."

As the confusion in Argentina continued, the invective against San Martín mounted. In retrospect it is so difficult to understand why. His marital relations were even attacked. Infidelities on his part, and even on the part of the now dead Remedios, were hinted at. As he was later to say, with the forthright bewilderment of a soldier, "In this war of the pen made on me, I cannot defend myself with the same weapon, as it is unknown to me."

Unable to stand the viciousness of the intrusions which were totally destroying what little tranquility was left him, San Martín made his final decision: self-imposed exile in Europe. He must leave America forever. He embarked for the last time on the long journey across the pampas. In Buenos Aires, he refused an armed escort provided by his few friends, who feared assassins might attempt to take his life.

One of his last acts during the brief stay in the city was to erect a simple tombstone over Remedios' grave. On it he had inscribed the words:

HERE LIES REMEDIOS ESCALADA
WIFE AND FRIEND OF GENERAL SAN MARTIN

Against the wishes of the family, he embarked for Europe with his seven-year-old daughter in February, 1824. He had determined to bring up the child himself. They lived for a while in Belgium and finally settled in Boulogne, in France.

The upbringing which San Martín gave Mercedes was a strange combination of love and rigid discipline. More than anything else, it perhaps resembled the care which a kindly old colonel might give a raw country recruit! Perhaps the expression which admonishes a parent to "spank a child a lot, but love it a lot" might apply. In any case, either because of the semi-military upbringing or in spite of it, Mercedes grew up to be a fine and loving daughter, the strength and comfort of her father in his old age. He arranged a marriage for her with Mariano Balarce, the son of an old companion in arms, General Balarce, who was the Argentinian Ambassador to France. The marriage was extremely happy; before long there were grandchildren to enliven the days.

During these last years the eternal problem was that of money to live upon. All the great promised pensions were not paid. The farm at Mendoza yielded nothing. There was literally money for nothing but food. Shoes were worn out, clothing was patched and bare. Occasionally, O'Higgins, also in exile, managed to send a few pesos to his old friend; occasionally the house in Buenos Aires, which belonged to Remedios, yielded small amounts of rent. Otherwise, San Martín lived on the charity and goodwill of friends. At one point he was ready to apply to the government of France for a place on its indigent rolls, but he was saved by a rare stroke of luck.

He was forced to walk everywhere, as there was no money available for cab fare. One morning he heard a voice calling him in the street. It came out of the far distant past and was that of Alejandro Aguado, a poverty-stricken officer comrade in the old days of the Murcia Regiment in Spain. Aguado had since made a fortune in the banking business. San Martín had often heard the name but had never connected it with his old friend.

Aguado insisted, without listening to any argument, that he be allowed to support San Martín. He bought him a small chalet along the river, connected by a pleasant bridge to his own mansion on the other bank. When San Martín protested, Aguado cried out, *"Hombre,* when one cannot be the liberator of half a world, one must be pardoned for spending the money one has earned being a mere banker. Say no more of it, please."

Eventually, San Martín no longer needed such kind and loving generosity. As he had hoped, later generations were kinder to him than his own. As the years slipped by, the calumnies and the vilification lessened and finally stopped. He was recognized as one of the great spirits of the age, and people insisted that justice be done. Chile restored him on her records to the status of a national figure and put him on the payroll as a general on active service. And to her great credit also, Peru made amends and rewarded him a pension for the services he had rendered.

San Martín's last years were vastly different from those of Simón Bolívar. The time passed in peace, in contentment, even in tranquility. His health improved; he long since had had no need for opium.

He took no active part in politics of any kind. He believed in man's ability to govern himself but, like Bolívar at the end, he saw the impossibility of it in the lands he had helped to liberate until the people had learned to forget their differences and had acquired the disciplines necessary for democracy to function.

He was saddened at the tumult in the Americas—from one end to the other: the loss of freedom, the collapse of public order, the swift trend toward dictatorship. But he took it more philosophically than Bolívar. He was more optimistic and felt that the new generations would somehow find the ways and the means to correct the excesses. San Martín never set foot on Argentinian soil again. Countless offers were made by revolutionary groups for him to come home and lead them. He never accepted. He would have been willing to return to take up a fight against an outside enemy, but he remained true to his vow never to engage in a civil war, never to dishonor his sword with American blood. He made one attempt to visit his native land, but when he arrived in Buenos Aires, he found the nation in the throes of a new, violent civil disturbance. He did not even go ashore, but continued on to Montevideo, in Uruguay, for a short stay. Old friends, old companions of the wars, implored him to remain, to help them in their struggle against what they called "the tyranny." He would have nothing to do with such uprisings, mistrusting them all, realizing that only through respect for law, law enacted by an elected body, would peace ever be established.

And so the years drifted past, peacefully. San Martín was grateful for the blessings which were his. He read, he wrote and he enjoyed his daughter, her husband and his grandchildren. He loved plants and all growing things, and even though Boulogne was not the place dearest to his heart ("rare and beautiful Mendoza"), he was content. In the garden of the little chalet, he worked and puttered to his heart's content. And more than pleasing to him, his home became a mecca for old comrades from South America. With the passage of more time it became a haven for the children of these old comrades. They came to visit, to talk, to sit in respect before him and to learn from the legendary old hero something of the truth of the times of their fathers.

José de San Martín died quietly in 1850, at the age of seventy-two. With him were those he loved best—his daughter, her husband and their young children. Years after his death, his remains were finally brought home to Argentina. Today his casket lies in state in the Cathedral of Buenos Aires, flanked by the stained and torn battle flags of the Army of the Andes.

Of all the keys to the character of this very great American, perhaps the best is to be found in a set of maxims which he penned as guides for the development of the character of Mercedes shortly after their arrival in Europe. They were stern maxims for a small girl, but they stemmed from the heart of her father; they had been the rules by which he had guided his own life for years, so she heeded them. These maxims today are printed in Argentina and are taken very much to heart by the schoolchildren of that country.

San Martín told little Mercedes to:

1) Be gentle, even to harmless insects. As Stern once said to a fly, "Go, poor creature, the world is large enough for both of us."

2) Love truth and hate lies.

3) Be inspired to love her father with confidence and friendship, but to respect him as well.

4) Be charitable toward the poor and unfortunate.

5) Respect other people's property.

6) Learn to keep a secret.

7) Respect all religions.

8) Be kind to servants, the poor and the elderly.

9) Speak little but to the point.

10) Have good table manners.

11) Despise luxury, love one's country, love freedom.

Of all the words written by San Martín, and of all those written about him, these perhaps express best the aims and hopes of his life. Certainly none written by anyone better express the spirit of this very great American.

SUGGESTED FURTHER READINGS

Belaude, Victor A. *Bolivar and the Political Thought of the Spanish-American Revolution.* New York: Octagon Books, Inc., 1967.

Cameron, Roderick. *Viceroyalties of the West: The Spanish Empire in Latin America.* Boston: Little, Brown & Co., 1968.

Desacola, Jean. *Daily Life in Peru in the Time of the Spaniards.* New York: Macmillan, 1968.

Mitre, Bartolome. *Emancipation of South America.* New York: Cooper Square Publishers, 1893.

Moses, Bernard. *South America on the Eve of Emancipation.* New York: Cooper Square Publishers.

Munro, Dana G. *Latin American Republics: A History.* 3rd ed. New York: Appleton-Century-Crofts.

Robertson, William S. *Rise of the Spanish-American Republics As Told in the Lives of Their Liberators.* New York: The Free Press.

Worcester, Donald. *Makers of Latin America.* New York: Dutton, 1966.

INDEX

Abascal y Souza, José Fernando, 140, 141
Aguado, Alejandro, 178–179
Artigas, José, 26

Belgrano, General Manuel, 53–54, 81, 121, 130
Beltran, Father Luis, 66–67, 91, 99, 118
Bolívar, Simón, 23, 58, 71, 100, 155–156, 157–169, 179
Bonaparte, Napoleon, 13, 15, 16, 39, 74, 113, 115
Bornos, Count de, 9

Cabral, Juan Batista, 49
Charles V (king of Spain), 171
Chilabert, Francisco, 40–41
Cochrane, Lady, 127–128
Cochrane, Lord, 126–129, 147, 151
Cortes, Hernando, 24
Cruz, Godoy, 137

De Alvear, Carlos, 39

De Güimes, General Martín, 57
De La Serna, General José, 75, 149, 151
De Olazábal, Captain Manuel, 174
De Vera, Francisco, 39

Epaminondas, General, 115
Epictetus, 79
Escalada, Don Antonio José de (father-in-law), 46

Ferdinand (king of Spain), 15, 16–17, 31, 72, 74, 142

Guido, Tomas, 81

Haigh, Samuel, 110–111
Hildalgo y Costilla, Father Miguel, 22
Holmberg, Baron, 40

Isabella (queen of Spain), 171

Joseph (king of Spain), 15

ABOUT THE AUTHOR

Paul Rink is a native Californian, born in San Jose in 1912, and now living in Monterey. In college he majored in science and in literature and subsequently went to sea for several years as an engineering officer on merchant and other ships. Mr. Rink has lived and traveled widely in Latin America where he engaged in the import-export business, was an engineer on a salvage ship operated by the Panama Canal and served with the United States State Department. During the years of work, travel and study, Mr. Rink wrote continually. His stories and articles have appeared in national magazines. He has worked extensively in documentary and semi-documentary TV as a writer and producer of network series programs. He is also the author of a number of biographies and non-fiction books for young people.